LIVE
YOUR
DASH

Make Every Moment Matter

LINDA ELLIS,

AUTHOR OF THE WORLD-FAMOUS POEM "THE DASH"

STERLING ETHOS
New York

STERLING ETHOS
New York

An Imprint of Sterling Publishing
387 Park Avenue South
New York, NY 10016

ISBN 978-1-4027-8729-4 (hardcover)
ISBN 978-1-4027-9089-8 (ebook)

Distributed in Canada by Sterling Publishing
$^{c}/o$ Canadian Manda Group, 165 Dufferin Street
Toronto, Ontario, Canada M6K 3H6
Distributed in the United Kingdom by GMC Distribution Services
Castle Place, 166 High Street, Lewes, East Sussex, England BN7 1XU
Distributed in Australia by Capricorn Link (Australia) Pty. Ltd.
P.O. Box 704, Windsor, NSW 2756, Australia

For information about custom editions, special sales, and premium and corporate purchases, please contact Sterling Special Sales at 800-805-5489 or specialsales@sterlingpublishing.com.

Manufactured in the United States of America

2 4 6 8 10 9 7 5 3 1

www.sterlingpublishing.com

To everyone who believed in me . . .

Contents

Introduction

Writers believe in their words and stories like mothers believe in their children. We mold them, we love them, and we send them out into the world hoping and believing others will love them too.

While writing this introduction, I overheard a weatherperson on TV referencing an incoming low-pressure system. I thought immediately how that phrase epitomizes the concept of this book. Though I've written a book that falls under a genre that identifies itself with labels like *self-help* and *growth and improvement*, I didn't want readers to feel as if this was merely another compilation of expectations, tasks, and "happiness assignments" that would add even more pressure to their never-ending to-do lists. Instead, I wanted to present a "low-pressure system" offering various deal-in-real options, ideas, and practical solutions.

Our conversation with happiness is a solo one—no one can tell us what we need to make ourselves happy. There is no cookie-cutter solution that applies to everyone. Deep down, each of us knows what he or she wants—or needs—to fix in order to live an enhanced and more rewarding life. My hope is that, in this book, you will discover reminders and aha! moments that will trigger an intuitive desire to recognize and repair what is broken and to eliminate the issues that are preventing you from freely moving forward and truly "living your dash"!

YOU DON'T HAVE TO BE SICK TO GET BETTER

Numerous self-help books line store shelves today boasting new and improved strategies for achieving "personal transformation." This is because so many of us are seeking a clear path that, this time, will minimize our stress, maximize our productivity, and aid us in attaining that ever-elusive "balance" between our personal and professional lives.

I've purchased my share of books based on "proven" life-changing programs and read many of their complex plans and elaborate strategies, fully intending to implement every step and chapter into my life immediately upon leaving the bookstore. However, after reading and earnestly adopting the first four or five recommended actions, I would inevitably become disinterested, lose my enthusiasm, and slowly wander back into my old, familiar, negative habits.

That is precisely why I wrote this book! In it are notable, quotable anecdotes and savvy suggestions that are not numbered, nor inextricably linked to one another. Each story, each poem, each life lesson stands alone. There are no chapters full of tasks to complete before you can move on to the next. Each story contains its own unique suggestion, take-away, or "dash" of inspiration. I believe the simpler the suggestion, the more easily it can be retained, remembered, and implemented into our daily lives. The purpose of this book is not to convince you to change your entire life in one fell swoop, but to integrate small, meaningful changes over time that, when combined, may create that "personal transformation." Yet, even if transformation is neither desired nor 100 percent achieved, isn't the end result still a better person? Aren't one or more positive changes in your life worth the time and effort?

Advice or suggestions offered should not compel someone to make a single "decision" to change. Change involves independent choices, whereas a decision is a pronouncement, a conclusion, a verdict. I prefer to use the word *choice* because a person who chooses to amend a habit or redirect his or her standard method of operating will be faced with that choice again and again throughout life. Making a decision, or verdict, creates additional pressure and a possible foundation for failure from the onset. For instance, when a smoker makes a "decision" to stop smoking, he or she will have to choose to remake that decision every time the craving for nicotine strikes. Instead, a choice is an individual, earnest, conscious intent to remain on a chosen path.

> *"You are always only one choice away from changing your life."*
> ~Marcy Blochowiak

During the more than fourteen years since I first put the words of "The Dash" poem together, I've had the opportunity to correspond with thousands of people around the globe, who, because they found a direct connection from my soul to theirs through my words, found it easy to share their innermost feelings with me. I've shared in the hopes, disappointments, happiness, fears, loves, losses, and life experiences of thousands. Though strangers, they have sought my advice, guidance, and sometimes nothing more than my heartfelt support. It's as though my words have created a virtual link between people all over the world and me. They hit a nerve with millions, and their inspiration continues to sink into hearts and minds like drops of water into a sponge.

I've learned more about life and living through the magic of these connections than I could have through any other educational avenue. I've learned about people—living, dying, giving, loving and trying to make the most of their dashes. I know of nothing else that could have better prepared me to write this book. My words have allowed me to get to know the inner selves of people better than I could have if I had been introduced to their outer selves first. Instead of reaching out to shake their hands through formal introductions, I've been given this opportunity to bypass external barriers and pretenses and—though we were strangers—to reach inside and touch their hearts. Therefore, the stories and lessons I offer in this book are based not only upon my life and my experiences, but also upon what I've learned and gained through theirs.

I believe if an author or poet writes with the intent to profit, rather than to inspire, the result is transparent to the critical eye of the reader, which can discern words derived not from sincerity, nor from the heart, but from desperate, empty pockets. My intent was to supply enough inspirational fodder for the reader to feed upon to hopefully grow and enrich his or her dash. If one reader identifies with some, most, or all of the distinct ideas and concepts included in this book and feels compelled to share his or her discoveries with others, I will honestly label my efforts a resounding success.

Live Your Dash.

Linda Ellis

The line etched into a headstone
between the dates of birth and death
represents each step we take on earth
. . . and every single breath.

To many, it is but a hyphen . . .
marking time between the years,
but in that little dash, is a lifetime
of laughter, love and tears.

We each create the legacy
our dash will someday represent
and decide if the life we're given
is truly lived . . . or merely spent.

Some deem themselves successful
if they can spend in large amounts,
but how you live your only dash
is all that really counts.

Because success should not be measured
in what you will buy, or own,
but in the pride you feel
in the person you're with
. . . when you are all alone.

Time steals our days and hours
before we recognize the theft
and we live each day not knowing
how much of our dash is left.

The responsibilities of daily life;
the bills, the job, the cash,
affect the way we choose to use
this important little dash.

Life uses special moments,
much like a poet uses rhyme
to engrave upon our hearts and souls
single, precious blocks of time.

We often overlook these gifts,
though we may not mean to do it;
we walk right past a special moment
instead of walking through it.

These memories in the making,
are happening now and happening here;
if we don't take the time to make the time,
they quickly disappear.

To experience each moment,
to laugh . . . to love . . . to live . . .
to learn just how much to take from life
. . . and just how much to give.

For when our time on earth is ending,
we won't remember every day,
but we will recall those moments
we chose to live along the way.

Consider your lifetime as a novel—
you, the sole author and creator,
writing and living every chapter
for those to read and cherish, later.

Will they say you lived your dash
with worry, stress and chatter
or know you seized
every chance you had to:
Make Every Moment Matter?

ON
SELF-REFLECTION

R.I.P.

I receive a large amount of e-mail asking from where many of my stories come, and if I truly "walk the talk" by following the positive themes in the stories I write. My answer is always the same. The story ideas come from my own daily life, my struggles, and my fears. A good actor often literally puts himself into the environment of a character he wishes to portray so that he is able to do so with genuineness and sincerity. If he is playing a convict, he will spend time visiting a prison. If he is to play a hunter, he may take lessons to learn how to properly hold a gun so as not to look like a novice in the film. The same strategy holds true for the ideas in my stories. If I haven't yet experienced the fears, hopes, dreams, and sometimes the agony of a particular aspect of life—through my own experience or through the eyes of someone else—I will not pen a story about it. And yes, I strive to live the positive ideals I write about, but no one is perfect. I'm sure fitness guru Richard Simmons has consumed his share of Twinkies.

Most people think of the acronym R.I.P. as representing the phrase "Rest In Peace," used most often when referring to lost loved ones and friends. That is exactly why I chose this well-known acronym, associated mostly with the end of life, to represent a simple theme to assist us in the living of life. I've transformed the acronym to represent the following:

RECOGNIZE, IMPLEMENT, PROCEED

Simply following the course of these three verbs, I believe, will lead to practicing the plain, powerful, positive suggestions I recommend in this

1

book. Recognizing, implementing, and proceeding are three vital ingredients in any recipe that offers suggestions to change our lives for the better.

RECOGNIZE:

- those imperfections or perceived weaknesses in yourself that you are able to so easily notice in others;

- the distance between who you are and who you want to be;

- the unnecessary pressures, deadlines, and commitments you needlessly—and often subconsciously—place upon your own life that have a negative affect on how you "live your dash."

IMPLEMENT:

- the changes necessary to convert those imperfections and weaknesses into strengths;

- the positive tools that will help bridge that distance between who you are and who you want to be;

- a thought process that will minimize, and often eliminate, the amount of self-induced stress you allow to filter into your daily life.

PROCEED:

- with honest self-reflection, conscious effort, and these newly acquired, easily-integrated tools to focus on what really matters in this temporary life and learn to take full advantage of the finite opportunities you have, but often overlook, to experience and live the moments of your dash.

Deal in Real

We are all going to die. Uplifting way to start an inspirational book, right? However, it often seems as though this truth has become some perverse secret we attempt to keep from ourselves. Death is our most common common denominator. It is the single bond that unites every living creature. It is what ultimately makes each of us a part of everything. Yet, the mention of the word brings incredibly varied reactions from people. We all know it's the truth, yet we are hesitant, mentally reluctant to embrace the reality. However, the truth is, the sooner we "deal in real" and face the fact, the sooner we can truly begin living our dash. I'm going to die. You're going to die. The cat lying on my feet while I write this, the blooming rose outside my window, and the woman who handed you coffee this morning on your way to work are all going to die. We cannot learn to appreciate the immeasurable worth and value of the life with which we have been blessed until we honestly realize and completely comprehend how utterly transitory it is.

Time is our best tutor, and the "fragility of life" realization comes with the territory of aging and maturing. Often this reality strikes our consciousness like a lightning bolt from a clear blue sky. Recently, I watched a combat marine speaking candidly in a documentary about his moment of truth. He stated how he had spent many months in intense training for situations involving various death scenarios. He fully believed he was committed and prepared to face and accept what could happen. Yet the reality only penetrated his mind and soul after he had lost a comrade within a few feet of where he stood.

The realization entered my own life after I'd read the words of a letter that had been routed around the office where I worked many years ago. The wife of an employee whose demise was imminent had penned it. I was so moved by her letter that I saved a copy of it and continue to live by her words:

> Regrets? I have a few. Too much worrying. I worried about finding the right husband and having children, being on time, being late, and so on. It didn't matter. It all works out, and it would have worked out without the worries and the tears. If I would have known then what I know now . . . But I did, and so do you. We're all going to die. Stop worrying and start loving and living.

Her words stuck with me. Her letter made me stop and think. *This is it. This is all we get.* It is an absolute, inarguable, and unfortunate fact that there will come a day when each of us will run out of tomorrows. Once we eliminate the residual effects of any hopeful ambiguity, and without the presence of morbid apprehension can openly discuss death as a reality—even if only with ourselves—true appreciation for life can begin.

The "deal in real" approach can be applied to almost every aspect of your personal or professional life. While this strategy may seem too blunt, the time and energy candor saves will far make up for any hurt feelings or misguided assumptions along the way. When we begin a project or goal by avoiding or eliminating unnecessary distractions, we can accomplish that goal without investing so much time and angst by using more honest—and because of that honesty, more efficient—methods.

It Is What It Is

Analyze: to separate (a material or abstract entity) into constituent parts or elements; determine the elements or essential features of (opposed to synthesize).

Huh? Even the definition of the word *analyze* is too analytical.

I agree with the necessity of analyzing world conflicts that prevent us from attaining world peace or the reasons behind an airplane crash, but when it comes to our everyday vernacular, the word *analyze* doesn't belong. More often than not, analytical views on simple matters are what make the proverbial mountains out of molehills. Sometimes, it "just is what it is."

A few years after moving to Georgia, I visited an analyst because I had developed a terrible—what some might call an irrational—fear of tornadoes. I'd assumed it was because when I was nine months pregnant I visited an elderly friend in a mobile home park during an ominous storm. I began to panic when announcers on the radio instructed us to evacuate immediately! Have you ever witnessed the attempted evacuation of three hundred residents of a mobile home park in a fifteen-minute time span? Positive I was about to become a mother right there in the middle of Hwy 92, I frantically searched for safe haven. My eyes perused the shopping center like a lioness searching for the weakest prey in a herd of wildebeests. Aha! A pizza restaurant! I thought that surely its faux-concrete walls would sustain the (what I had convinced myself was a) category F4 storm that I believed was about to inflict its full force on the two-foot area that surrounded me. (Hence the words *irrational fear* . . .) But they wouldn't even let me in! Here I was, a crazed, angry pregnant woman pounding on their door with clenched fists. I can't imagine *WHY* they wouldn't open it! Later, I discovered to my dismay that stores and restaurants in the area had locked their doors and secured their immediate perimeters, anticipating the oncoming line of twisters.

In the weeks that followed, I tried to forget the incident and ignore my unreasonable behavior during the storm. However, I just couldn't shake the memory of how I'd reacted, and I was fearful I might act the same way the next time dark clouds came my way, as they surely would. I tried in earnest to explain my fears to a prominent mental healthcare professional:

Linda: "Doctor, I'm deathly afraid of the wind in these mini-cyclones."

Doctor: "I believe your fear stems from your family breaking apart at a tender age and the significance of that crossroad in your life . . ."

Linda: "No, with respect, I'm pretty darn sure it's the wind."

Doctor: "It's the family foundation . . . it was torn apart . . . and you long for that union to be intact once again . . ."

Linda: "No . . . uhm, it's the wind."

Doctor: "The damage a tornado wreaks represents the damage to your early psyche due to your broken home."

Linda: "NO . . . IT'S THE WIND!"

A large percentage of what makes up our fears and phobias stems from ignorance: that which we do not know for certain, or haven't taken it upon ourselves to learn. When I realized this, I began to deal in real more often. I started reading about tornadoes, watching documentaries, and facing and examining dark clouds when they'd appear in the sky instead of turning to run. I considered the true odds of a tornado striking my home in particular and researched how many tornadoes, compared to the hundreds that have hit my state through the years, had wreaked havoc in my town specifically. I literally felt my fears dissolving. The more I understood and learned, the less I feared. I had eliminated the element of ignorance from my fear (that of the unknown) because I'd made it known.

After living most of my life in the south, I still respect tornadoes. Except now, instead of gathering every person, animal, and inanimate object that means anything to me, including the toaster, a stapler, a box of dog biscuits, and the dustpan (hey, you never know what you'll need in an emergency) and heading to the basement every time the wind blows, I concentrate on the facts and deal in real.

Most solutions are reached far more easily when we view the facts at face value. The more variables and justifications added to an issue, the longer the distance becomes between the problem and the answer.

Among other fears I'd discovered as the years began to accumulate was a fear of dying, and of death. One by one, my grandparents left this Earth, and my fear kept me from attending even one of their funeral services, something I regret to this day. However, lessons I had learned from my father about living . . . eventually taught me about dying, as well. In time, I was able to face the actuality of death, as he had—realistically. He was a mechanic by trade and viewed life with a "find what's broken and fix it" mentality. Rather than hypothesize, he would deal in real. When he found out he had a cancerous tumor, he wanted to know the location, the size, and what other organs it inevitably would effect. He would spread medical journals and diagrams of the human body out on his living room floor and, as I watched his innate ingenuity come alive, I quickly began to understand his intent. I witnessed how he viewed the similarities between a working machine—an engine—and the human body. He wanted to fully understand, in mechanic's terms, how the body's "engine," "transmission," and "carburetor" worked in conjunction with each other. And as his organs (or engine parts, as he viewed and referred to them) began to fail, he understood why and what to expect next. He prepared himself by eliminating the fear of the unknown. I watched and learned as he literally fragmented and removed his fears of death, while unknowingly removing mine as well.

Advise Yourself

Some people say hindsight is 20/20, but the magnification on the invisible bifocals we wear while singling out others' foibles and faults offers unmatched clarity. Additionally, we are baffled when others do not seem to have the capability to see their own (what we believe are blatant) weaknesses as clearly as we can, neither do they share our eagerness to quickly rectify them. In addition, how is it that our bifocals are subconsciously removed when we turn to focus on our own blunders and limitations?

Most of us take great pride in the advice we carefully dispense to friends and family. We listen, we evaluate, we attempt to resolve their problems. But in fact, the definition of a true friend is not someone who solves others' problems. More often than not, those who share their concerns with us are seeking guidance and support, not absolute solutions. They often require nothing more than resonation: when they hear their own words speaking the pros, cons, and facts of a dilemma, the answer becomes crystal clear. Succinctly put, they are more in need of an ear than a mouth.

Regardless, many times while we are offering a sympathetic ear, we are simultaneously probing our brain for an unsolicited solution. We can effortlessly pinpoint the crux of a quandary and readily offer advice and a solution—when it is not our own.

When it comes to your own problems, the solutions may be very easy to find. If instructions and recommendations for others emerge from your mouth as easily as candy from a Pez dispenser, chances are you have in your arsenal the greatest possible weapon to combat your own foes and woes: your own advice. As close as any friend or loved one might become or however well he or she may know you, it is impossible to know you as well as you know yourself. For many of us, our first instinct when troubles arise is to seek someone else's opinion or counsel. However, we don't stop to realize that we often already know the answer to our problems before unburdening our heart and soul. In the pretense of searching for guidance, what we are truly seeking is validation. We offer both sides of the issue to our empathetic listener in hopes that their views will match our own. In fact, to ensure this, we will often seek out those who we know will share our particular point of view.

The best option would be to clone ourselves and, therefore, create perfect, customized, problem-solving individuals. These clones would know us better than anyone, share our opinions and views, donate their focused and undivided attention, and provide impartial opinions lacking judgment or attitude. In addition, we would know for certain that they have only our best interests at heart. However, we all know that's impossible . . . or is it?

It's been said we are our own worst enemies. Following that same point of view, why can't you, in turn, be your own best friend? Before turning to another person for assistance—unless what you're seeking is purely a physical sympathetic embrace—check in with yourself first. Before laying all your cards out on the table, assess what you have in your hand. Prior to adding your troubles to someone else's burdens, consider advising yourself. Compare this strategy to that of "having an inside connection" or getting the "inside scoop." The most direct, honest, and effective information you can find comes from that which is closest to the core.

———

Stand in front of a mirror. Speak your mind . . . to your mind. As we learned in elementary school, *s o u n d* it out. Have a conversation with yourself. Trust your instincts and rely on your own natural resources. If and when you've exhausted every viewpoint and option, you find yourself still longing for an outsider's view (everyone, except you, is an outsider, no matter how close you are)—then, and only then, fill that need. However, keep in mind the deception of the old cliché, "he knows me better than I know myself." Deal in real. *No one* knows you better than you.

Inside Accessories

Every day we groom and primp ourselves in order to improve our outward appearances. We shower, we shave, we fix our hair or put on makeup. Our vain attempts are performed in order to become more appealing to the eyes, those of the beholder and those of the "court of appeals" from whom we receive silent judgment each day.

Initially, we seek approval from ourselves as we examine the image reflected from the mirror—our "outside me." While some are content to satisfy their view of themselves, many have instead adopted a primary objective of winning the admiration of others. We spend many hours every week preparing and perfecting how our image will be seen. However, that image, no matter how coiffed, limits what we are able to display to the world. Yet, maintaining it often becomes a higher priority than working on beautifying who we really are—the me that is not seen through sight—the "inside me."

We adorn ourselves in an attempt to improve how we are perceived in the eyes of those we encounter every day. We coordinate our clothing and accessories as though putting together an outfit is a compulsory task. We shop for accessories and dangle, pin, clasp, and clip them to our hair, jackets, wrists, necks, arms, fingers, and ears, all in an attempt to dress up our outside "me." What would you add each day if people could see your inside me as well? What accessories would you choose if you could shop somewhere to prettify, decorate, and garnish your inside me to make it worthy of others' approval before stepping out into the world? If a mirror existed that would reflect your attitude, outlook, and mind-set, would you like what you see? Would you be proud to display it to others, unadorned? What would your reflection need? How would you accessorize your inside me to raise the level of pride and confidence you feel in yourself? Would you add the inside accessory of kindness, of generosity, of compassion? Would your inside image lack consideration, empathy, or patience? What inside accessories would you eliminate from your reflection—greed, arrogance, conceit? Envision that image glaring back at you. If your true ideals were displayed there in the glass, how would that picture make you feel?

Live Your Dash.

INSIDE OUT

Does your inside match your outside?
Does your outside match your in?
Do the kind deeds you envision
stay confined within your skin?

Your thoughts and your life's actions—
are they close . . . or far apart?
Is the way in which you live your life
what you believe deep in your heart?

Are you the same person on the inside
people meet on the out,
or do the two clash and differ
leaving your conscience full of doubt?

Do you change to fit each circumstance
like a chameleon changes hues
or honestly communicate
your true beliefs and views?

Do you turn your back on your ideals
when it seems they're not in vogue
and follow the path of least resistance
instead of boldly going rogue?

Have you learned from all the lessons
life has taught you as you've grown?
Do you respect the person you are with
when you are all alone?

Do you praise yourself for goodwill
that is only in your head?
Can you replace "do as I say, not as I do"
with "do as I do," instead?

Are you a different person
than the person people see?
Are you a different person
than the one you'd like to be?

In you, can others place their trust
and never be deceived
and see you as you really are,
not how you wish to be perceived?

Would they not see a difference,
or would they grieve in sorrow,
if your inside today
became your outside tomorrow?

WYSIWYG

YSIWYG (pronounced "wizzywig") is an acronym for What You See Is What You Get. The term is used in computing to describe a system in which content displayed during the editing process appears almost verbatim to the final output.

E-mails are sent around the Internet displaying before and after pictures of beautiful celebrity women. Without makeup and accessories, their outside appearances would classify many of them as merely "plain Janes." In a state of WYSIWYG, without the glitz and glam, we realize more easily that they are people with scars, imperfections, and problems.

A few years ago I had a very important speaking engagement scheduled and went shopping for an appropriate ensemble. However, that day was a harried one, and I did not dress to match the ambience of the stores I would be frequenting. I didn't take the time to put on the mask of makeup I've learned to hide behind. Like many of my usual Saturdays, I went WYSIWYG.

It was immediately apparent that I wasn't as welcomed as I had been during my previous visits to these stores, when I'd arrived fully matched and coiffed. Although it didn't matter to me much, I could see that the assumption was that someone appearing in this upscale shop wearing a baseball cap over a ponytail with an obvious hole in her jeans would not have carte blanche, a gold card, or an unlimited clothing budget. Unfortunately, customer service was nearly nil for me that day, and in return, I left without purchasing one item.

I've begun to experience a profound metamorphosis as the years evaporate before my eyes. I am currently feeling a strong inward desire to go back to basics and tap into my own natural resources. I find myself hiding less behind mascara masks and artificial fingernails, in direct opposition to every concept conveyed in commercials for age-defying products. I had always thought that my yearning for products that disguise wrinkles and fade laugh lines would increase, not decrease, as the years progressed. Although, like many women, I still comb my eyelashes with black globs of gook whose ingredients remain a mystery to me, I now carry out the routine far less often, and only as my career necessitates. I've discovered that beautifying the outside me takes time—my most precious natural resource—and I find myself less willing to relinquish this precious commodity to inconsequential habits. The crash diets have ceased. I now spend my time making my house appear acceptably clean, instead of attempting to make it look as though no one lives here. I am now spending more of my dash performing a far more gratifying ritual: dressing up the inside me.

Automobiles are equipped with tachometers, speedometers, and odometers, which measure rotations per minute, speed, and distance traveled. What if other inanimate objects in our lives had instruments to measure their usage? What if our mirrors contained vainometers to measure how many times we inspect our "outside me" each day? Would we consider ourselves vain, insecure, or a little of both if the gauge gave a high reading?

When my oldest daughter was an infant, we were involved in an auto accident caused by a woman who had not yielded the right-of-way to oncoming traffic. In addition to the damage to our vehicle, my knee sustained injuries. Due to the financial constraints of a young working mother, I sought monetary assistance from the at-fault driver's insurance company to help with my medical expenses. The physical pain from the injury finally faded, but the lesson I'd learned from the experience remains to this day.

Seeking legal guidance, I spoke to an attorney. I shared the news that the orthopedic doctor had recommended I undergo surgery to correct repeated displacement of my patella. The response I received from the attorney astounds me to this day. He replied, "That's good. Scars pay more." When I asked him to explain further, he told me that surgery was considered one thing by the insurance companies, but a medical settlement would be more substantial if I was left with some sort of permanent disfigurement on my body, albeit minor. In other words, I could have pain and suffering to organs inside due to internal injuries, but if the world could plainly see that the "outside me" was affected, I would be better compensated. He eagerly encouraged me to have the surgery, but I'd detected his reasoning was derived from an entirely different type of *compa$$ion*. I thanked him for his "concern" and hung up the phone.

Whether his words had anything to do with my decision, I'll never know. I opted not to have that surgery. I'm not the type that a scar would have bothered me psychologically, but the reason behind the decision to have that surgery would have, every time I wore shorts.

As a society, we put far too much emphasis on appearances. Take the heart, for instance. The heart has been used as a representative of the spiritual, moral, and emotional core of a human for years. Poetically and symbolically, it is used to denote adoration, compassion, caring, and of course, love. However, the sight of a heart (a rather unattractive organ) was unappealing, and because it had been chosen somewhere down the line to represent love and romance, it had to be altered. (There are other vital organs that could have been used to represent love instead. Though I suppose the lyrics, "*I left my liver in San Francisco,*" or the cliché, "*He wears his lung on his sleeve,*" may not have sounded as endearing.)

Because the (ugly) heart was designated as the organ of compassion and feeling, apparently it had to be transformed into a cartoonish graphic. Why wasn't it left in its original form to be printed on anniversary cards and Valentines? Because people want to like what they see on the outside! For the same reason, beautiful furniture is often constructed using inexpensive particleboard filler. The outside may be beautiful oak wood veneer with intricate natural wood designs, while the inside is nothing more than a material that rates one step above sawdust. People are attracted to the attractive . . . that which pleases our eyes. We have become accustomed to believing that outside appearances are what are most important.

Technically speaking, a greeting card should resemble this:

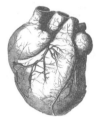

However this image is far more appealing:

We are so conditioned that those of us who are not cardiologists instinctively think of the stylized image when we refer to the heart. Furthermore, we have come to believe that we suffer a "heartache" when unfortunate things happen. In actuality, it is the brain that processes the details of sad events, and it is from the brain that we derive our sorrow. So in essence, we are experiencing the effects of "brain pain," not heartache.

FIRST IMPRESSIONS

How many people are in your life right now that you thought about negatively when you first met them? Did you grant them a second, third, or fourth chance before you made decisions about the type of person they were? How many of these people, did you find out later, thought negatively of you from the first impression? Though it's true you never get a second chance to make a first impression, those who base their future relationships with you on their first impressions may prove, more often than not, to be ultimately not worthy of concern.

We must remember that things aren't always as they seem during a first impression. There are always two sides to every story. When my two daughters were younger, we took them to an outside function at a nearby park on a summer afternoon. While sitting in the chairs facing the stage, awaiting the performance, a light rain began to fall. Anticipating the change in weather, I'd brought along two umbrellas, one for my daughters and one for my husband and me. However, my youngest daughter had not yet mastered the art of sharing and decided to hold the umbrella directly over her head, leaving her sister exposed to the elements. After repeated requests and fairly stern admonitions, she refused to share the comfort of the dry space underneath the umbrella. As a parent, sometimes you take advantage of such opportunities to teach valuable lessons. After awhile, I reached over and took the umbrella from her and handed it to her sister, which left her blonde locks suddenly uncovered. I thought a little light rain falling upon her stubborn head might do some good. A few seconds afterward, a well-meaning but meddlesome couple sat down in the chairs behind us. Having not been privy to the events occurring before their arrival, I grinned as I overheard them commenting about the sweet little girl sitting there in the drizzle. (Oh, what terrible parents would do such a thing!) Furthermore, they offered their umbrella to my daughter, who, never missing an opportunity, replied in the sweetest of tones, "Oh, thank you. Thank you very much."

DO NOT BELIEVE IN FIRST IMPRESSIONS,

FOR THINGS AREN'T ALWAYS AS THEY SEEM.

SOMETIMES THE VERY SMALLEST PLAYER

IS THE BEST ONE ON THE TEAM.

"I" Infection

Often referred to as the "Me Monster," or linked to the phrase "Me, Myself, and I," I have dubbed this common condition the "I Infection." Perhaps just a simpler view of narcissism, I have defined it as a state of mind based upon a primary focus, first and foremost, on one's own issues, problems, needs, and feelings. This, in combination with a dedicated belief that one's life load is—in every possible instance—heavier than that of his or her neighbor's, creates an "I Infection." Though I don't believe this concocted condition has been identified in any medical journals to date, I can tell you that it is treatable and curable once behavioral awareness has been established. (You might call such treatment an "ant-I-biotic.")

The symptoms begin with a tendency to publicly focus on oneself by forcing any given topic of conversation to execute a 180-degree turn away from the speaker to what the infected consider home base—their life, their issues, their concerns, and their problems. To validate the reason for this rotation, they "add" something to the topic, thereby elevating interest in the story by making it worse, better, or simply ranking it higher on an achievement scale than that which is being spoken.

The most notable sign of someone suffering from this ailment is an attitude that appears to lack compassion, empathy, and/or an innate concern for others. I say "appears to," because that is how those who are inflicted with an I Infection appear to others, though I don't believe that is always the case. An apparent lack of qualities such as compassion and empathy does not necessarily signify that they are completely absent. To treat this affliction, the sufferer must first begin with recognition and then admission, followed by a sincere desire to correct the problem. Recovery will follow shortly afterward.

The I Infection arises from a strategy left over from childhood. Children have a strong and consistent desire to draw attention to themselves, and many adults are happy to oblige, believing that offering undivided attention and praise may help build confidence and self-esteem.

Two arguments can be made for those who suffer from an I Infection in adulthood. One might say they received too much reactionary adoration and attention as a child and now, as an adult, expect it from others. On the other hand, one could argue they didn't receive enough desired attention as a child, and, therefore, seek it from others. Regardless, it is an instantly noticeable and undesirable affliction.

I Infections are, unfortunately, extremely difficult to recognize in ourselves but immediately obvious when we encounter others who have contracted this condition. Furthermore, the contagion can spread, as the more the "patient" proclaims his or her superiority, the more innocent participants wish to squelch this obnoxious behavior by immediately reacting. They soon find themselves engaging in the sport of "one-upmanship." Two people with I Infections can become oblivious to their surroundings as they spar for the spotlight, the attention of each other, and the title of Main Focus of Everyone Around Them. I once saw a comedian speak about this condition. He said you could instantly distinguish the Me Monsters in a crowd by stating that you have recently had a wisdom tooth removed. They will immediately respond with, "Oh . . . I had all FOUR removed last year . . . at the same time . . . and . . . I was in bed for days . . . and . . . " Instead of allowing you to finish your story, the conversation becomes like an arrow catching a tail wind, suddenly pointing to the person with the I Infection, who now intentionally commands the conversation.

The ability to listen attentively is one of the most admirable, sought-after attributes anyone can possess. It's an art. It's a trait. It's a gift. Having or being a friend who listens is a great treasure in itself. But *truly* listening involves much more than an occasional "uh-huh" and a random nod. I've read articles from conversationalists who recommend repeating sentences that someone has said to reaffirm your interest and validate that you are indeed listening. It is not such a great strategy for those afflicted with an I Infection, however, because they will seize the opportunity to switch focus from the speaker to themselves. They will view this sort of interruption as a torch they have been handed, which enables them to take over the conversation. Unbeknown to the original speaker and any listeners, they will become the new speakers by redirecting the conversation to their stories, their lives, their experiences.

The first step in curing an I Infection is to recognize the symptoms. This involves a focus on listening attentively (instead of enthusiastically) and learning to add more silent nods, rather than interjecting. Silence and eye contact are far more effective in letting someone know you are listening and you care. Listening is something innate, yet most of us can learn to do it better. Randomly interjecting your personal experiences into a conversation does not confirm that you are listening but that you believe what you have to offer is better, worse, or more entertaining. Rather than proving you are listening and interested, it proves you are processing and planning while someone is speaking.

Have you ever been put on the spot by the question, "What do you think about that?" after you have failed to provide your undivided attention to a friend's recollection of an event? Did you attempt to respond with a cover-up answer that only displayed the fact that you weren't listening attentively, digging yourself into a deeper hole? Being a friend who half attempts to offer caring, undivided attention is worse than being a friend who admits he or she cannot.

We've all met people who suffer from an I Infection. Are you thinking of family and friends who fall under this category? Do you recognize any of the symptoms in yourself? Are others silently thinking you suffer from an I Infection? We are often unknowingly turned into self-focused people from the results of hurt, pain, stress, and responsibilities. Slowly, our lives begin to revolve primarily around our needs, our issues, our feelings, and our problems. When we allow our lives to become so busy that indifference replaces compassion, we subconsciously stop listening to others. The inevitable outcome is an unfulfilled life based on self-focus, self-centeredness, and self-pity. When we open our ears to truly listen to each other, we simultaneously open our hearts. Listening was one of the first things we did as humans. It is how we've learned . . . it is how we've grown. To regain focus on our priorities, we need to hone this fundamental trait.

Would YOU Choose YOU?

Are you the friend to others you believe yourself to be? Do you give more than you take from relationships? Do you possess the qualities you seek or admire in others? Think about this question honestly: If you were given the opportunity, knowing all that you know, would you choose you as a friend, confidant, spouse, or companion?

Many of you will be driven by your own egos to answer that last question with a resounding yes! However, are you being completely truthful with yourself? You want your friends to be thoughtful. Are you thoughtful? You want your companions to be trustworthy. Are you worthy of their trust? You want your family members to be caring. Are you there to offer them love and compassion when they need it most?

If you hesitated answering the "Would you choose you?" question, why? Are you not the type of person you'd like others in your life to be? Do you not possess the attributes that you prefer your friends, family, and companions to have? Is that acceptable to you, or do you wish to fill the gap between who you are and who you'd like to be?

If you were asked to write a short list of adjectives that you would want people to choose to describe your dash after you leave this Earth, and then to write a short, honest list of adjectives you believe people would use, how would they compare? What small things can you do today to ensure the two lists align with one another? Maybe you could call an old friend, offer an apology, be more generous, forgiving, and helpful, perform A-OKs (Acts of Kindness), smile more, complain less. Whatever tasks or improvements you feel would fill the gap between who you are and who you want to be, you can begin applying them—today.

Happy Rebirthday!

It is often said that today is the first day of the rest of your life. From this point forward, begin making changes to your dash. Don't make the decision to think about it next week, or add another to-do task to your list. Just begin at the beginning. Nothing is stopping you from starting to integrate change the next minute of the first day of the rest of your life. First comes the choice. Make the choice now.

IF EYES WERE MADE OF MIRRORS

AND I COULD SEE WHAT OTHERS SEE,

WOULD THE REFLECTION BE WHAT I BELIEVE

OTHERS SEE IN ME?

ON
HAPPINESS

Getting Ready (to Live)

hat two verbs, which are opposites, have you performed and will continue to perform—simultaneously, every single day of your life—since the day you were born? Inhaling and exhaling? Walking and running? Smiling and frowning? No, you can't do any of those at the same time. The answer is living and dying. Right now, you are living while you are dying and dying while you are living. It is up to you which act gets the most consideration.

"I can't die now—I haven't been happy yet . . ." Do you live in a perpetual state of getting ready to live? Getting ready to live is not living. Have you fallen into a cycle of using today's minutes planning for tomorrow, and tomorrow's minutes planning for the next? If you are the kind of person who requires visuals, planning tools, directions, and a scheduled task in order to begin something, then write the following phrase (in ink) across today's calendar box: **"Start living!"**

In most cases, to "start" something, you need to speed up something else. So it may seem somewhat convoluted, that to start living, you will need to do the opposite: slow down. I've often used the metaphor of a speeding passenger train to describe this process. While the train is speeding, the view from the window is nothing more than a blurry hue with no definition. You cannot identify individual sights, be awed by their splendor, or focus and appreciate all that is passing you by. However, as the train begins to slow down, the view becomes much clearer, and you have time to identify and absorb the essences of life. Haste does indeed make waste.

I grin whenever I hear the phrase, "It seemed as though time stood still . . . " No, it didn't . . . YOU did! Time only stands still in photos, the only known entity capable of capturing a moment in time.

IF WE CHALLENGE THE CHAMPION OF TIME,

THROUGH THE BOUT, WE WILL SURRENDER

AS WELTERWEIGHTS AGAINST THE TITLE;

NAUGHT BUT A SHAMEFUL, WEAK CONTENDER.

MY FOUR D'S

Since my forties have been my most enlightened decade thus far, I thought it would be appropriate to use a Four-D's strategy to assist me in actually living life, instead of always getting ready to live it.

Disengage: To begin moving forward, I knew I had to disengage from what was holding me back. I learned that sometimes it takes a temporary escape from living the life you are living in order to step back far enough to see the whole picture and reevaluate your priorities. By practicing mental disengagement from my negative behaviors, I made room to engage more positive ones in the future.

Decelerate: In order to focus on the world around me, I had to lose the pace that was causing my blessings to become blurred. By moving too fast, I was missing too much. I had to ease up on the accelerator long enough to recognize the person I'd become, compare it to the person I want to be, and pinpoint the areas that needed improvement in order to bridge that gap.

Decline: While honing my life skills, I had to weaken my people-pleasing skills. Though it saddened me at times, I had to learn how to politely decline requests of my time, energy, and invitations. It was I that, over time, had branded myself the Queen of Everything. I was striving to be everything and everywhere for everyone. When you give too much to too many, it affects the quality of what you have to give. I had to realize that the word *No* is a complete sentence.

Decompress: Definition: to bring (a person exposed to conditions of increased pressure) gradually back to normal. By practicing my Four-D's in my forties, I was able to decompress and begin living following a slower, more relaxed pace. By decreasing the pressure, I was able to focus more, give more, and live more.

SATURDAY THINGS

Though times have changed dramatically with increased innovation, the regular "workweek" used to be considered Monday through Friday. Saturdays were reserved—reserved for enjoyment, reserved for experiencing life outside of the workplace.

However, the busier our lives became and the more responsibilities that were piled upon our shoulders, the more the leftover tasks from the workweek began to invade our Saturdays. Saturdays of enjoyment have slowly transformed into Saturdays filled with odd jobs and errands that could not, for one reason or another, be completed throughout the workweek. Saturdays often become nothing more than an extension of the workweek . . . filled with duties.

Whenever I start stating aloud all that I have to do on a Saturday, my husband responds, "Make a list." I hate lists. I have a list in my phone, a list on the notebook at my desk, a list in my computer, and a perpetually unwritten list floating around my head twenty-four hours a day. I've had to create an LOL—a List of Lists—just to keep track of my lists!

I've decided recently to choose random Saturdays throughout the year to become totally listless. I don't mean listless as in lethargic or lacking energy. In fact, it's quite the opposite. I say "listless" literally, as in to be without a list. I've been known to wake up on a Saturday, jump into my car without a destination, and drive, leaving my lists behind. I call them spontaneous acts of freedom. It is a bit of an oxymoron to say one can be simultaneously listless and energetic, but by adding freedom and exploring new avenues without a list to guide my every action, I've added creativity, enthusiasm, and fun back into intermittent Saturdays. I look forward to my listless Saturdays, as they are no longer days simply filled with leftover tasks and errands but filled instead with impromptu, unplanned, spontaneous . . . life.

LIFE'S CALLING PLAN

Have you seen the cell-phone company commercials that state that their calling plan is better than a competitor's because their minutes "roll over"? Wouldn't it be wonderful if life worked that way—if we could only use the minutes of the day we'd like and let the others roll over into the next day, week, or month? Unfortunately, however, we all know that life's "calling plan" doesn't offer rollover minutes, and our only option is to use them or lose them.

So why not make the most of the "unused" minutes in your day? If you're stuck in a dentist's office awaiting your appointment, strike up a conversation, bring a good book, take an interest in your surroundings. The other day I sat in a doctor's office and studied the birds they had on display in a cage. I found myself completely involved in their environment, and saddened that they were imprisoned. I wondered how a bird could cope with such frustration—being blessed with wings and freedom and having those blessings revoked simply because someone admired his plumage and unique idiosyncrasies. I compared their predicament to my need for anti-anxiety medication, which I took just to calm myself enough to spend thirty minutes inside an MRI machine. I found myself wondering if these flightless birds had access to tiny bird anti-anxiety medications. Fortunately, as my thought process digressed, my name was called, and I went in to see the doctor.

It's a matter of where you find yourself—not psychologically, but physically. The people and things at the specific places where you are, at the specific times you are there offer opportunities to learn, to grow, to make the most of where you find yourself. You can gauge quite easily if your counterpart on the sofa at the vet's office has an approachable personality. If so, begin a conversation, ask questions, and make a new friend, even if only temporarily. If that person is not receptive to friendly conversation, refer to the QTIP theory (Quit Taking It Personally), and engage yourself elsewhere to pass the time. When you find yourself walking down a street, smile, wave . . . inhabit the moment. When you're on a plane, occupy your "now" and don't just endure the experience—make the most of it.

Life offers us beautiful moments to recognize, but do not cast aside the "unmoments," because they fill our lives as well. Accept the peaks and valleys, highs and lows, ups and downs. The rhythm of their inconsistencies is the very pulse of life. Learn to move and dance to that rhythm and once again realize the joy in enjoying. Make the most of the minutes in life's calling plan. Have a love affair with life! Wherever you find yourself, be there.

LIVE LIKE YOU ARE ~~DYING~~ LIVING

We've all heard the popular phrase: "Live like you are dying." Stories are written about the concept, songs have been recorded based on its message, and the phrase has become commonplace in sermons, speeches, books, and inspirational columns. But . . . what does it mean, exactly? Does it translate to the implication that you should live like you are dying, tomorrow? Next Thursday? Next month?

The obvious intent of this five-word wannabe epiphany is to imagine you have been offered some dismal news from your doctor and have a limited time to mend fences and complete a "bucket list" of things you wanted to do but never got around to completing in life for one reason or another. The underlying message is that we should be doing what we are mentally postponing. Of course, the phrase is not practical in its literal sense, because if we truly learned that we would be dying soon, we might quit our jobs, start eating cheesecake for breakfast, and go lounge on a beach somewhere in the Caribbean. If doctors guessed the expiration dates of moderately healthy patients, a more likely scenario might be that your doctor would enter the examination room and state something like: "I've got some news for you . . . you have forty-one years to live . . . "

So, why not convert the essence of the phrase to represent reality, and say: "Live like you are living!" Because you are.

"What's important is how frequently you're happy, not how intensely. Those peaks of happiness—getting swept off your feet, scaling a mountain top, winning a bundle in Las Vegas—are nice, but happiness comes down to being quietly content most of the time."

—Dr. Joyce Brothers

RESISTING A REST

Have you convinced yourself that *filled* (*packed, crammed, crowded*) means the same as *fulfilled* (*satisfied, content, pleased*)?

Do you consider staying perpetually busy, living?

Have you subconsciously melded the two opposite scenarios, making a living and making a life to the point at which you can no longer differentiate their meaning?

Do you equate being constantly active or productive with living a satisfying and rewarding life? Does guilt overcome you when you find yourself spending idle time?

Do you believe that because you can be doing something planned or constructive every moment, you should be?

Nothing is wrong with doing nothing occasionally! It doesn't mean you're being lazy or unproductive, and it won't change your life forever. When a tool that is battery charged begins to run low on power, it needs its energy supply replenished. It needs to be recharged, or it is useless. So it is with our bodies. There are times, besides when we sleep at night, when they need to recharge, to restore, and to replenish. The body, mind, heart, senses, and spirit need uninterrupted time. It's as though, in the back of our minds, we have created imaginary Time Police who will step out and issue a warrant if we don't resist *a rest*. The pressure we put upon ourselves to fill every waking hour with activity is palpable. The guilt we feel during and after spending idle time may be blamed on life's pressures, but it is created only by us.

THE DUMBWAITER

Have you been waiting to put forth effort toward reaching a goal, hope, or dream? What are you waiting for? Are you waiting for validation from others? Are you waiting for the perfect scenario? Are you waiting for a sign? Are you waiting for a change in your current living situation or surroundings? Are you waiting for the planets to align in a specific pattern or for hell to freeze over? Whatever it is, if you're waiting for outside influences to make positive changes in your life while time ticks away, you're a dumbwaiter. Dumbwaiters appear to be, on the outside, just living to die . . . but inside, they are just dying to live.

During one of the positions I held in the corporate world, I had the privilege to meet and befriend a man who was one of the most honest and respectable I've ever known. After many devoted years with the same company, he looked forward to his retirement with an almost zealous anticipation. He spent his time planning, dreaming, literally living for the day of his retirement. He lived prudently, investing a majority of his money, year after year, into a retirement fund. Eventually, he bought an RV to travel the country with his wife. He would spend hours mapping out routes to destinations they'd planned to visit. At last, the day arrived. The company gave him a huge retirement party with all of the predictable gifts and goodwill sentiments. However, his dreams were cut short when, not long after his retirement, he suddenly passed away.

Life continually offers us lessons, if our minds are open to recognize, accept, and learn from them. It is wonderful to be passionate about our dreams and goals, anticipate them, and plan for them accordingly. However, it can prove to be a costly mistake when we waste the majority of the time we have now literally living for tomorrow.

"Life is what happens to you while you're busy making other plans."
—John Lennon

Live Your Dash.

"The Day Between"

Yesterday will never reoccur;
tomorrow cannot be foreseen.
The only thing that matters
is the day found in between.

The past and the future
fill too much of what is me
with memories and emotions
of what has passed…or what might be.

Anticipation and regret
seem to gnaw at my soul
until I'm wrapped in a cocoon of days
that I cannot control.

Though one is gone forever;
its seconds slowly ticked away,
and I was never promised
a day after today.

The present is a perfect blend
of what I've done and where I've been.
I have never been this old before,
nor will I be this young again.

Today, I made a solemn vow
only to myself
to place yesterday's regrets and woes
high upon a shelf . . .

unreachable and out of mind
will be that stress and sorrow
alongside their companion;
the worries of tomorrow.

I shall escape the chains that bind me
to what I cannot rearrange
for what will be . . . will always be
and what was . . . I cannot change.

My heart will then embrace its freedom
The here and now will matter more.
I will inhabit my life's moments
like I never have before . . .

by realizing everything I have
instead of what I lack
and letting go of all the obstacles
I've allowed to hold me back.

The hours I've lived
and those still pending,
whatever they may mean,
cannot compare to the magnificence
of the day found in between.

The Smile Connection

Asmile; a simple curvature of the lips. We each take our smile for granted, though it is the most powerful, free tool for communication we have at our disposal. A smile is an instrument that crosses international boundaries, a unique mediator, an icebreaker, and a facial beautifier. Its side effects are more potent than any prescription medication. The immediate reaction a smile produces is natural and automatic. Even forcing a smile can affect your mood, your attitude, and enhance your appearance.

The power of a smile became evident to me last month as I lay directly under a starry southern night sky. I rested my head back on a pillow in my hot tub and gazed above me. Instantly, I noticed a unique cloud formation, outlined as clearly as if it were the product of a talented graphic artist in the sky. It was a perfect smiling face, and it was skewed at just the right angle to be staring directly down at me. The irony was that my instant, subconscious reaction was . . . to return the smile! It took me a moment to realize what had happened. It was an instinctive response. It was what my face automatically does, without my permission, when someone smiles in my direction, but it was a warm exchange, and it felt good, at least until I realized I was sitting alone in a hot tub wearing a big goofy smile directed at a cloud.

I realized that evening how much a smile represents an instant connection—a recognizable gesture, a common link. To some of us, smiling comes as naturally as breathing. Often, we don't even realize we are doing it. A genuine smile has the ability to change a preconceived opinion or break the tension in an uncomfortable situation. However, it's not only your mouth that smiles—your eyes smile as well when you form a genuine smile. As an experiment, look into a mirror with a serious look on your face, with only your eyes in view. Then smile. You can see in your eyes, without having a view of your mouth, the difference a smile makes. A smile is the passport kindness uses to travel to your eyes, your heart, and your soul.

A smile can cross every language barrier without miscommunication. Its intent is instantly recognizable and rarely misconstrued. I was visiting a salon recently at which the women, both the management and personnel, did not speak any English. However, through motions and smiles, the English-speaking patrons there, including me, were communicating our requests more than adequately. Then something happened: The manager of the salon was on a telephone call speaking fast and fluently, in her native language. Apparently, her friend on the other end of the line told her a very funny joke, because she began to snicker, which turned into a giggle that soon mushroomed into a bellowing, hearty laugh. The effect of watching her smile and laugh until tears were flowing down her face spread through the room like a viral contagion. Before we knew it, we were all enjoying a moment of hysterical laughter, and at what . . . we had no idea! Her smile, her laughter, and her warmth shone through so brightly that we felt compelled to share the enjoyment, though we never really knew why. It was as though for those few minutes, we all spoke the same language.

I smile frequently. I smile at strangers. I smile at people I know aren't going to smile back. Why? Because it is a part of who I am. I've also learned that not being a smiler doesn't make someone a terrible person, and that many people harbor reasons and resentments that prevent them from smiling often. I've learned that, for some, it is difficult to smile if you have experienced extreme pain and disappointment in life. I've learned that people use their facial façades as a gate. If they smile, they feel they are opening that gate to an unwelcome world. They don't believe, as I do, that sharing a smile is like aspirin for the soul. It helps remove the hurt, from the inside out.

Why are so many people afraid to smile? Do they believe it exposes vulnerability? Does it make them more approachable when they want to remain distant? Some feel that smiling eliminates the invisible wall they have constructed between them and the world. I say, what's the harm in doing that now and then? You can't win a ballgame by always playing defense.

Though the true meaning behind a smile is sometimes hard to detect and can often be misleading when it is used to mask insincerity, a genuine smile can turn someone's day around. It is a most powerful signal, and its meaning stands out from all other emotional expressions. Often, all it takes is a smile and words need never be spoken.

I once had some professional photos taken for publicity purposes. Afterward, I sat in the studio for ninety minutes waiting to view my "instant" photo proofs. As I sat, repeatedly repositioning myself in a chair with no arms and silently admiring the handbag of a customer seated nearby, I overheard the sales woman (whose nametag should have borne the title "Flattery Manager") speaking to a customer.

Apparently, this company had figured out that showering customers with adulation regarding their photos, including, "Oh, look at that beautiful smile" and "Your eyes look so bright and attractive in this one" had a direct impact on its quarterly profits. (I guessed that this particular employee had recently completed the "Catapulting Compliments to Increase Sales" section of the company's training manual.)

Then it was my turn. I was seated in front of a large screen as my photo slideshow was displayed with accompanying background music that, if it had contained lyrics, would have repeated one chorus: "Buy this photo; it flatters you. And while you're at it, buy this one, too."

However, I had my defenses up, prepared to hear the empty praises aimed more at my checkbook than the truth. As my pictures began to fade in and fade out, I waited for the trained Flattery Manager to tell me how "beautiful" the expression was on my face, or "what a great hair day" I was having, as I'd heard her say to the previous client. So I was surprised when I heard the particular adjective she had chosen instead to describe my photos. She studied each picture and then thoughtfully turned to me and said, "Your smile is so . . ." I anticipated the word she was going to select as a sales tactic out of hundreds of potential candidates: *pretty, attractive* (or even *straight* or *white*!). But no, she used the highly underestimated adjective *CONTA-GIOUS* to describe me! "Contagious?" I replied, partly disappointed that I didn't receive my inflated compliments and partly curious as to why she had chosen that particular description. I thought to myself, "Maybe she meant *congenial* or *considerate*, or even *consistent*!" I asked for clarification. "*Contagious?*" I inquired once more. Her nod confirmed the trait she had detected in the expressions captured by the camera's lens. Then another sales woman approached and concurred, "Yes, she is contagious!"

Hmmmmmm, I thought . . . *Well, okay. I've got a contagious smile. I can deal with that. It could be worse.* Granted, the word did not encourage me to write a bigger check for more photos, but it did get me thinking. Later, I even looked up the word, whose figurative definition is: "likely to spread to or affect others . . . transmittable . . . transferable."

Suddenly, I realized that *contagious* was indeed a complimentary character-ization, even though I'd only heard it used previously in negative terms. In fact, it was one of the most sincere, flattering compliments I'd ever received! I'm glad I'm contagious! Although I didn't plan to repeat that aloud in a crowded room or elevator, I vowed right then to become even MORE contagious!

Furthermore, I think it would be a nicer world if everyone displayed a smile or an attitude worthy of being branded *contagious*. I briefly had visions of single-handedly starting an outbreak of a bug the medical profession would call the "Amicable Virus" that would spread like an epidemic and infect millions! It would be a plague transferred through smiles from person to person on airplanes, in traffic jams, in lines at the grocery store . . .

Though I may have gotten a little carried away with my newfound attribute, I still intend to proudly continue to "infect" everyone I meet with a "contagious" smile and a positive, "communicable" attitude. Practice being contagious more often and witness the profound effect it can have on the people in your world!

"Whoever is happy will make others happy, too."
—Anne Frank

Filters

When we look in any direction, we have the opportunity to view hundreds of different objects in various sizes and colors. Yet, we choose only a small percentage of them to fixate on during any moment in time. By using an invisible filter, like a sieve with a million tiny holes, we automatically divide items into two sections: that which we choose to view clearly and that which is in view peripherally—the leftovers.

All of our senses become involved as we filter an immense quantity of random incoming data in order to prevent sensory overload. Using our filters, we create our own world inside the world at large. Naturally, what you choose to create as your world, and what I use to create mine will differ immensely, though we may have the same options from which to choose. We can filter our thoughts. We can filter our memories. We can use filters to determine what is allowed in, which ultimately forms our opinions and our attitudes.

Will your life be better when remembered through a filter? Probably, but does it matter? What harm does it do, as we grow older, to focus on the good, the happy, the joyous, and the cheerful moments of our lives? We don't have to forget the negative memories. We can just put them in the archived files of our minds . . . way in the back . . . under some boxes . . . in a darkened corner . . .

Just as we are able to filter how we retrieve what is stored in our memories, we can filter how we perceive reality on a daily basis. Last winter I applied a filter that turned my attitude, and my day, around. A few weeks after experiencing our first white Christmas since the 1800s, we were, according to news reports "paralyzed" by a record-setting snowfall here in Georgia. Not being as equipped for such an onslaught of the white stuff as our neighbors to the north, local businesses, major interstates, colleges, and schools were closed, mail delivery was halted, and all the dismal weather predictions contained the same word: *ICE*. Our winter storm had arrived at a particularly bad time for me as my company was expecting to receive and send overnight checks and packages and had to cancel a scheduled meeting. Although the beauty of the snowfall was breathtaking, its splendor did not surpass its inconvenience.

After hearing news reports of how the storm had crippled the south, I stepped outside to assess the damages personally. I sneered at the gray clouds and knocked the ice from the deck railing with my fist. It seemed to give me some satisfaction, watching it crack and crash to the ground. It was a crucial week for my business, and this storm would certainly cost me time and money. That afternoon, I'd received e-mail from business associates who were experiencing the same angst over the cessation in productivity. We had plans, a schedule to follow, and deadlines to meet.

Just as I rested my elbows on the deck railing to hold up my aching head, Zachary, the ten-year-old boy who lives next door, came bounding around the corner of the house. Visualizing his face today, I'm not sure I can remember another time when I witnessed a smile that wide. I watched him as he scooted his boots through the snow with determination and designed an intricate series of tunneled tracks through the yard. He shouted with obvious delight and both arms stretched up in the air: "School's closed tomorrow!" Then he picked up a uniquely shaped sheet of ice from a nearby snowdrift, peered through it as if it were a glass pane, turning it in different directions, and yelled with exuberance: "LOOK at this! Isn't this GREAT?" He bent to pick up a handful of untouched snow and swallowed it like ice cream. He spoke excitedly about the things he had seen, what he had done, and all that had happened. His eyes were dancing with the thrill of it all.

Initially, I felt what I thought was a curious pang of jealousy. *Of course he can afford to be happy*, was my initial thought process. *He has no deadlines, meetings, or expected packages. He is free to just enjoy.* Instantly, I saw the contrast in black and white. I was hit with the honest truth that, though we had both witnessed the same events, I hadn't seen them unfurl in the same way he had. It was as though we were experiencing different realities, simultaneously. Why hadn't I just accepted the circumstances I was powerless to change? Why hadn't I decided to make the best of a situation and relish the fleeting moments, instead of using them to complain? Yes, Zachary, there was fun to be had, and a winter wonderland to absorb. Times like these are few and far between in the South, and the brakes had already been applied to my busy schedule.

I quickly grabbed my hat, scarf, and gloves and walked through the backyard. I threw a ball for my dog and watched her cheerfully romp through the snow. I made an attempt at creating what resulted in a small, oddly shaped snowman with bits of pine straw sticking out from various parts of his head and torso. I strolled slowly as I watched a design emerge on either side of the walkway in response to my lengthy footsteps. I took pictures of the snow sitting ironically upon its unaccustomed hosts, the fronds of our Sable palm. I watched the light glistening off the ice that had formed like crystal spears on the roof's edge, pointing directly toward the ground. The sight of them brought forth a recollection of stalactites I'd seen in caverns as a child on vacation. Then I smiled as I watched the birds hopping ever so quickly upon the frozen ground in ill attempts to find small, writhing meals atop the ice. I filtered in only the positive, and by doing so, I decided how the event would be experienced and later remembered. I chose to see the world initially, as a child does, through a filter of optimism, which lets in the good, the joyful, and the positive first.

"The truth is, we see in life what we want to see. If you search for ugliness you'll find plenty of it. If you want to find fault with other people, your career, or the world in general, you'll certainly be able to do so. But the opposite is also true. If you look for the extraordinary in the ordinary, you can train yourself to see it."
—Richard Carlson, PhD

Day Labeling

Your alarm clock didn't ring on the day of an important meeting, you stubbed your toe on the way to the bathroom, and you stumbled downstairs to make coffee and proceeded to spill it all over yourself. You repeated aloud, "THIS is going to be a bad day." The way some days begin, you feel like adopting the mantra of Norm from the show *Cheers*: "It's a dog-eat-dog world and I'm wearing milk-bone underwear." Maybe that's partially true—trouble is inevitable. It's the misery that's optional.

It doesn't have to be a bad day. Start it over. I'm not suggesting that you literally start over by going back to bed, resetting the alarm clock and avoiding the bedpost. I'm simply suggesting it is best not to label the day. Continue your day from this point forward, without the label. When you put a label on a day, either in the morning or midway through, you are setting a tone for the day in your mind. By doing so, you are convincing yourself that, because the day started out in a less than desirable way, it will continue to spiral downward. And it will—if you allow it. However, you can turn it around at any time, using your most effective tool: your attitude. The first step is realizing it was your reaction to each situation, not the situation itself, that created the reasons behind your anticipation of a "bad" day.

I've often read the quote, "Every day may not be good, but there is good in every day." Why can't every day be good? We are the only ones who can make that choice, based on our reactions to negative stimuli. How far into a previously labeled "bad" day do you begin thinking, "I cannot wait until today is over!" You are wishing away perfectly salvageable hours that you might ultimately yearn to have back someday. By mentally affixing a negative label to the day because of one or more unfortunate events, you help to satisfy a self-fulfilling prophecy. If it turns out in the end to have been a "bad" day, it was because you made it that way through your own interpretation of reality.

Is it time for an attitude inspection? It's easy to convince ourselves that we are going to have a bad day from the onset. The problem with day labeling is that once we accept the conclusion that a day is not worthy of anticipation or enthusiasm, that attitude can—and often will—sabotage and redirect the rest of the day. It's comparable to a placebo effect, when a percentage of patients in a study are told that they have been given a pain reducer, though it is nothing more than a sugar pill. Often, they will report feeling a reduced level of pain after taking the medication. They were expecting and anticipating pain relief in their minds from the pill they had swallowed, and in some cases, they received it.

Basically, if you expect bad things to continue to happen, based solely upon the fact that some already have, you are more susceptible to making that scenario a reality. In addition, keeping yourself in that initial mode of negativity may cause you to interpret even the positive as negative, because that is what you've decided to expect. Don't create your own pattern of bad. The result of one minute does not indicate the outcome of the next.

To be happy is not a decision that's made,

but rather a choice of joy over sorrow.

Today, you can choose to be happy, not sad

and wake to make the same choice tomorrow.

Forgive . . . and Forget?

The first can be accomplished much easier than the second. Many times we can forgive others easier than we can forgive ourselves. Other times, we can accept an apology, offer verbal forgiveness, feel that forgiveness in our hearts, but subsequently have a difficult time forgetting the transgression upon us. The question is, should the act of forgiving automatically offer complete absolution, or does it require an important part of the process—forgetting—to be completely executed?

Just how does one forget about bad things that have happened? How do you simply remove something that's rooted deeply in your mind? It seems the simple act of concentrating on forgetting something results in bringing more focus to what you are attempting to forget.

Someone once told me I should try a visualization type of therapy that would help me eliminate moments of pain, disappointment, and failure from my mind. I was instructed to mentally blow the incident into an imaginary balloon, tie it tightly, and envision the wind carrying it and my troubles far away as it disappeared high into the sky. This didn't work for me. In my visualization, the balloon hit a telephone wire, and the pain, disappointment, and failure was then transferred directly back to me through fiber optics!

I then tried my own version of "eraser therapy." When I was younger, I had a favorite toy called an Etch-a-Sketch. It has a red plastic frame with a gray screen in the center. The inside is filled with some type of sand, that as a child, I was convinced that this substance had magical qualities. An ingenious yet simple toy, the knobs on the corners turn in both directions and "draw" images through the sand, which then appear on the screen. Then, when your picture is finished (or, as in my case, when an obnoxious older brother devastates your artistic endeavors), the toy is turned over and shaken. When you flip it back over, the picture has disappeared, and you have a clean slate upon which to create yet another masterpiece.

I tried to mentally draw unpleasant occurrences from my life onto the screen, and then turn the toy over in my mind and shake it to erase them, representing their removal from my memory. I watched them disappear, lost inside the magic sand of the Etch-a-Sketch. However, in my visualization, the knobs starting turning by themselves (apparently as magical as the sand), and my unpleasant memories appeared as clearly as I'd first drawn them.

My friend was not surprised that my attempts had failed. He asked me to visualize a red box representing a blended combination of miscellaneous negative occurrences in my life. Then he asked me to try hard to forget about the red box completely. I tried to use an eraser in my mind to erase it. I tried to mentally burn it. I tried to obliterate it in ten different ways. The more I tried, the more I saw the red box when I closed my eyes. The harder I concentrated on eliminating it from my mind, the stronger the image became. I tried to use diversion therapy, and began purposely thinking of other things to forget about the red box. I thought of an elephant. I thought of the beach. Of course what followed was the thought of an elephant riding the waves toward . . . what else? . . . a big red box on the beach. I discovered it was nearly impossible for me to forget something on purpose.

I have heard many inspirational speakers and random professionals talking about how we need to learn from life's lessons, even the unpleasant ones. In the same breath, they recommend that we leave the past behind us and move on. I started thinking, how is it possible to do both? If we do manage to forget, and thus leave behind an unpleasant incident from which we've learned a lesson, aren't we leaving the valued lesson behind as well? How can we move on with our newly learned lesson in mind while simultaneously forgetting the entire incident from which it was acquired?

I've found that the secret is not to attempt to forget the entire incident but to separate it and take only the good parts with you. Take the lesson.

Leave the details of the pain. I fell down the stairs last year on Christmas Eve. Now every time I descend the staircase, I hold the handrail securely. I don't dwell upon the memory of the broken ankle and relive the entire experience—I hold the handrail. I took the lesson forward and left the negative details behind.

We can do the same with forgiveness. We can forgive and then forget the negative aspects of an unpleasant incident, while holding onto the lesson and bringing it with us as we continue our journey. We can let go of the fault. We can let go of the regret. We can let go of the blame. And we can hold onto the lesson.

Rear View Mirror

We all know that dwelling on harsh details is not healthy. Learning to leave the negative aspects of disappointments and failures behind us is important. I like to use this analogy: think of the size of a windshield. You look through a windshield so that you can move ahead, move on, move forward. It is very large. Then imagine the size of a rearview mirror. It is much smaller in size. This is where you should view your past failures and disappointments. Put them behind you as if viewing them from this mirror. See them as distant images that slowly fade, because it is the view from your windshield that is more important . . . it is your future, awaiting your arrival.

Senses Six and Seven

We all know about our "five" senses, those that most experts consider the most notable avenues of perception: our sense of hearing, sight, smell, touch, and taste. (Though I have read that there is no certain agreement among neurologists as to the number of senses, because the definition of what constitutes a sense can differ from expert to expert.)

Over the years, we learn to rely heavily on our senses. We are conditioned by our senses. A dog will eat a piece of paper that had been previously wrapped around a cheeseburger because of his senses. I put my hands over a flameless candle recently, and I could have sworn I felt a sensation of warmth.

I'd like to unofficially add two more senses to the top five. The sixth sense I propose is one we use every day, not unlike the original five. This sense is one that deserves more, but receives less, recognition. This sense is that feeling we have in our gut when we choose, or choose not, to do the right thing. The sixth sense is our conscience.

We are confronted daily with the choice between doing what is right or what is wrong, and every decision we make is based on the result of a feelings fight. To do the right thing, we must have this internal argument with our conscience, and we must emerge the victor. We fight feelings of greed, we fight feelings of hatred, we fight feelings of intolerance, all in an effort to do the right thing. Those who claim they never feel the emotions in a feelings fight are not worthy of praise, nor scrutiny because they deny experiencing them—they are worthy of recognition because they have learned to overcome them, to immediately do the right thing without question or hesitancy.

I've often wondered how some people can justify certain actions. I've come to the conclusion that these actions, which seem unjust and motivated by negative emotions, are often what results from the loss of a feelings fight. Worse yet, never having the internal brawl occur. As you age, your conscience begins to have a voice. A voice that represents the metamorphosis of insightful words from parents, teachers, and advisors through the years into what is today, your voice. It is the voice of who you are, when no one is watching.

I AM FOREVER PRESENT,

RESIDING IN YOUR HEAD

SILENTLY PERSUADING YOU

TO DO THE RIGHT THING, INSTEAD.

And Sometimes...You Win

Last month, I decided to take a chance at our weekly lottery drawing. As I stepped up to the kiosk to select a form, I saw a lottery ticket, topped with the silver dust leftover from previously scratched off options. It was apparently a losing ticket someone had left behind. I started filling out my form when I again glanced over at the ticket. I mentally added up the boxes and peeked over at the target number, the total those boxes was intended to exceed, to win. It was higher than the target number. It was a winning ticket. Math not being my strong suit, I added it up again, and again, but it came out a winner every time.

I picked up the ticket and walked around the immediate area with every intention of returning it to its rightful owner. No one was around. I thought about returning it to the Customer Service desk but imagined them announcing, "Whoever lost a winning lottery ticket, please come forward." I shrugged my shoulders and decided that wasn't going to be my best option. I then experienced a feelings fight. The "prize" of the ticket had not yet been revealed because obviously the ticket's owner was not a math genius either. I wrestled with the thought of cashing in the ticket as my own. I walked to the counter, ticket in hand, but I put the ticket in my pocket and turned away. I walked back to the section where the lottery forms are kept and began selecting my numbers to play.

Within a few minutes, an elderly man, assisted by a cane, walked to the automatic lottery ticket-dispensing machine near where I stood. I peered around the corner at him. I couldn't help but notice he had selected the same ticket game as the one in my pocket, out of about ten or more choices. He slowly made his way to the lottery stand where I was and began to scratch his ticket . . . in the same spot where I'd found the winning ticket. Maybe I've watched too many *Law & Order* episodes, but from this circumstantial evidence, I'd decided in my heart—this had to be the winning ticket's owner.

I began a conversation with my fellow gambler and asked, "Do you play scratch-offs often?" He answered curtly: "Yep . . . all the time." Through further attempts at niceties, I'd discovered that this was a curmudgeonly man who was in no mood to make cordial conversation. He was obviously on a mission to win money that afternoon. Still, even with his less-than-polite demeanor, and my mere circumstantial evidence, I was determined to return the winning ticket to its rightful owner.

I asked him, with as much false ignorance about the lottery scene as I could muster, how "this" particular game was played. The solution to my dilemma was in his answer. After he had explained the "rules," I realized he had completely misinterpreted the game. I took the ticket out of my pocket and tried to explain, but he answered quite rudely, "No, no, no. I've been playing for years. I know what I'm doing." At this point, Mother Teresa herself would have cashed the winning ticket. Yet, I kept trying.

"Sir, but doesn't the total of these numbers have to be greater than this number to win?" I asked. Obviously annoyed, he finally decided to give my idea some thought. "Well," he answered. "I guess you're right." Satisfied with myself, I asked if he had been playing this game earlier today. When he answered yes, I asked if he had left a ticket here at the kiosk. He answered, "I left a ticket there, but it was nothing but a loser." "Actually, I don't think it was," I responded. As innocent as I could appear, I pointed to the numbers on the ticket and added, "Doesn't this and this and this, add up to nine? And doesn't that beat the target number?" "Well, I believe it does," he said as he snatched the ticket from my hand and limped quicker than he had arrived over to the Customer Service desk to redeem his winnings.

I had performed an Act of Kindness, yet it was unusually unfulfilling. I had listened to my conscience and done what I felt was right, but something was nagging at me. Did I expect a show of gratitude? Maybe. Was I curious as to the prize he had won? Possibly. Was I regretting my decision? No.

I began my grocery shopping through the store and there on Aisle 8 was the old man. Walking alongside his wife and holding on to the shopping cart for support, he was wearing a grin from ear to ear. He paused a moment and whispered to me: "My wife says I spend too much money and time on those darn things because I never win. But I tell her it's not in the winning; it's in the fun and the thrill of playing. And, sometimes . . . you win." With that, he winked and walked away. There. I had it—the take-away from my good deed: the quote that made me smile all week, all month. It was the lesson that justified the loss.

Live Your Dash.

No Regret

At certain times I've envied those
with no uncertainties or doubt—
those who do not miss the guilt
they freely live their lives without—

making hasty, strong decisions
without ever looking back—
believing they are born leaders;
others merely are the pack—

ignoring feelings without care
while en route to their goals—
crossing bridges of success
while others pay their tolls . . .

for when they finally lose
everything that they have bet,
with an untapped conscience, they play again
with no remorse and no regret.

THE SEVENTH SENSE

The seventh sense I'd like to propose adding to the main list is a sense of humor. It would be the one sense that everyone uses and benefits from, albeit in vastly different ways. It is defined as amusement provoked from a particular cognitive experience, but it is so much more than that. Perhaps it was omitted from the chosen five because some people appear to have been born without it? However, since this sense becomes apparent on different levels, dictated by personal taste, it may only appear to be lacking in some, because that which one finds funny, another may deem strange, distasteful, or irrational.

People of all ages and cultures respond to humor. It is said that laughing can lower your blood pressure, reduce stress, and trigger the release of endorphins, our natural tranquilizers and pain relievers. Laughter is a vital source in our body's never-ending goal to reach and maintain an overall sense of well-being. Therefore, I would label it as the sense that makes the most sense.

Sometimes our body begins to laugh without us, without our knowledge or approval. These are the most satisfying laughs to experience. I remember an incident involving my father, who had a temper, attempting to lift a BBQ grill from a deck that was about four feet in height. He was trying, from on the ground, to reach up, grasp, and carry a grill that had been sitting all winter, to a lower deck so that it could be cleaned. I watched, bewildered, from the backyard as the top of the grill began to teeter like a seesaw, spilling its disgusting contents over the top on either side. I thought silently, *this could end in disaster* . . . and yet, I said nothing. When I look back, I wonder if I stayed silent in fear or in anticipation of the greatest laugh of my life.

I stood watching the event unfold and can recall the moment in detail in my mind. The thought of it still makes me laugh to this day. Just as the tray, which carried months' worth of nasty, stagnant liquids, tipped and cascaded over my father's head, I ran backward about twenty feet to ensure that I was safely removed from the scene. Initially, I stood shocked and motionless. I heard words in the distance I'm not sure I've learned the meaning of since. There may have been fumes of anger emanating from my father's ears, but

I couldn't see through my tears. I fell to the ground holding my stomach, laughing. I choked. I cried. I coughed. I can still remember the feeling in my stomach as it laughed uncontrollably, as if it were a separate entity not connected to my body. Though my sympathy for my father's situation was great, I simply could not hold back the laughter. I wasn't happy that it had happened to him, and I didn't really think the situation was funny, per se. But, knowing him well, and seeing him flailing his arms, cursing, and spitting because of an act he himself had committed, involving consequences he hadn't thought out fully, just tickled my funny bone like nothing ever had. My apparent disregard for his circumstance did not help the situation at all. It only made him angrier, which only served to make me laugh harder. However, I was only able to laugh because I knew my father was a person who could laugh at himself, and would . . . after his shower. I will never forget that day or retelling the story with him by my side during the thirty years that followed.

SILLY PEOPLE

Millions of people take themselves and their lives too seriously. They refuse to acknowledge the absurdities found too easily in everyday life. Being able to laugh at yourself means you have a priceless ability to put things into proper perspective. I am by nature a Silly Person. It's been a struggle for me to find the fine line between professionalism and silliness in my business, because through the pomp and circumstance and legalities, inside, I'm often laughing. I add humor to e-mails, speeches, conference calls. I've reached the point in my life at which I'd rather try being myself, even though at times it may appear that I am less experienced or less knowledgeable simply because I have a tendency to prefer fun and try to find the lighter side of most situations.

I also prefer to spend time with Silly People. They laugh more. They ignore more of life's inconveniences. They criticize others less. They are typically friendlier people. I love when, by happenstance, I am seated next to a fellow Silly Person on a plane or at a function. Silly People have an instant connection, like smokers or football fans. There are instant attributes one Silly Person knows another Silly will possess. The boundaries of conversation are more lax, and there is an instant feeling of relaxed comfort and ease. Stress of the unknown is reduced between strangers the sooner they realize they are both Silly People. In addition, we Sillies are easily recognizable. We are usually wearing a particular item referred to as a smile, and we proudly try to exude an aura of good-natured feelings.

LIGHTEN UP

I despise the word *immature*. More than once, I've seen the fear of being branded by this word stop folks from experiencing the times of their lives. When I think of the people in my life, both currently and those with whom I have crossed paths during my journey, my favorites are those who some might consider "immature"; those who refuse to allow their ages to dictate their attitudes. I call them the Old Kids.

We "immature" people are those who add salt to life. On my daughter's eighth birthday, I enlisted the assistance of a neighbor's daughter. We bought more than seventy-five balloons and some helium tanks, filled every balloon, added different lengths of string, and tied each to a separate weight. Balloons filled both sides of the street on either side of my home shortly before the arrival of the school bus. We had literally created a wall of greetings to welcome my daughter home from school on her special day. Though it didn't thrill the school bus driver when he had executed the turn onto our street, my daughter was beaming when she stepped off the bus. It is a moment neither of us will ever forget.

My favorite line from any movie is from Dudley Moore's *Arthur*, when he inquires enthusiastically: "Isn't fun the BEST thing to have?" Are you having fun regularly in your life now? Do you spend your time wishing, planning, and dreaming of how and when to have fun again? You don't always have to plan fun. You can find ways to infuse bits of fun into even the most mundane situations. For instance, when someone asks you what time it is at five after three, answer with, "It's 2:65."

Being free to have fun is fun itself. Set yourself free. Stage a mid-life crisis, if applicable, no matter what your age. If you have had one, have another! Those who perish younger than the "average" estimated old age are denied a mid-life crisis. We never really know where the middle is, do we?

"If we weren't all crazy, we would go insane."
—Jimmy Buffett

Ask yourself this question: How old would you be if you didn't know how old you are? Do you let your changing appearance dictate your attitude? If looking older is casting its spell over your feelings and actions, think of a dog. Dogs act like puppies as long as they possibly can . . . until only their body rejects their behavior. Stay as young in your mind as you feel in your heart. Don't let your age always dictate your actions. Don't let practicality always win over frivolity. When was the last time you had fun? If you took more than a few seconds to answer, it's been too long.

The entire year I had turned forty-five, I thought I was forty-six. I still don't know how this happened. I suppose monitoring the ages of my kids, spouse, friends, dogs, and cats caused me to lose track of my own. I discovered that there is a profound difference in the psyche of those two ages. Turning from age forty-five into forty-six (in my mind) was as much a milestone as turning from twenty-nine into thirty. Looking back now, I can see that I had begun to experience a change in mentality. I lived that year like I was four years from fifty, when in actuality I was six years from thirty-nine. I let the number dictate my actions. I cut my hair shorter and I began to think and act differently.

Marketers and advertisers prey on our weakest reality—that life and youth are temporary things. We are victims of a constant bombardment of advertisements and products that focus primarily on preserving our youth and hiding our age. From hair dye to wrinkle remover, they slowly try to view aging as not only undesirable, but unattractive. Many people believe there is life after death. I'll settle for life after youth.

GRAVY BOAT

"Paper or plastic, ma'am?" I glanced around in back of me to my left. I glanced around in back of me to my right. I was searching for the older woman to whom this young gentleman bagging my groceries must be referring. I shrugged my shoulders and swiped my ATM card and he repeated, "Paper or plastic, ma'am?" Obviously, the poor woman he was trying to catch the attention of had a hearing impairment as well. Because the only other female within a six-foot circumference of the checkout area was the cashier, I discretely scanned her attributes to determine her level of maturity and decide if she was indeed worthy of the label, "ma'am."

Like a boulder falling from a cliff, it hit me. This young gentleman was speaking to me!! "Paper!" I replied indignantly. (I usually choose plastic, but suddenly I wanted to display my defiance.) THAT would show him!

The many "milestones" like this that occur during life's journey serve as unintentional awakenings. We may coast through our forties and fifties with the same youthful mindset, while the shell that hosts and houses that mindset moves on with time. Those with whom we cross paths infrequently (and those who apparently don't seem to care whether or not they receive a sizeable tip) have only a brief opportunity to view our outward appearance. I've often wished, therefore, that there was a way to turn myself inside out. (Though, a visualization of the metaphor in this instance is rather grotesque, the analogy is definitely worthy of consideration.)

The most memorable age-awareness moment for me had been sitting still, patiently waiting to strike, on a shelf in my pantry. I was busy moving items around to put dishes away when I spotted it and stood motionless for what seemed like an eternity. It was a gravy boat. I stood there staring up at it intently. It was as though it was staring back. I asked myself, when . . . when did I become a gravy-boat owner? When did this happen? Grandmas own gravy boats. Do I even know how to make gravy? While I was reevaluating my life, my existence, and all that was me, I tried to think of where the time had gone. At what point did the responsibility of gravy-boat ownership become mine? When did I grow up?

There are much more significant, obvious indications of maturity, such as marriage, buying a home, having children, etc. However, these rites of passage that occur as we proceed from decade to decade, though smaller in stature, can have a similar, substantial impact on your consciousness. For some, it can be the realization that Froot Loops and Cocoa Puffs cereals no longer excite their palette. For others, it might be the first polite offer from a young person offering an available senior discount. For many, it is the discouraging awareness that silliness has slowly, surreptitiously been replaced by responsibility. For me, it was the gravy boat.

FOREVER YOUNG

Though I'd planned to grow old beautifully
with grace, dignity, and finesse,
as my brain remains suspended in time,
my body continues to progress!

I felt somewhat separated
and psychologically detached
when I realized I'd surpassed the age
when my mind and body matched!

The years that have advanced
with a slow, predictable rhythm
apparently left my mind behind,
but took my body with 'em!

As my heartless mirror reflects the years,
I've come to the realization . . .
that my attitude has opted
to join a younger generation!

Is this due to a lack of maturity?
Could I be completely wrong . . .
to think my body went and aged
without bringing me along?

It's like my age and my maturity
have been running a race,
and if the latter could accelerate,
it would still be in last place.

Though they used to run together
and were the best of friends,
I guess in the middle of middle age,
is where this courtship ends.

I admit my youth has faded;
it just seems as though time took it,
but I do not intend to act my age . . .
just because I suddenly look it!

ON
SUCCESS

Definition of Success

My first experience entering the realm of public speaking was to address a large audience comprised of professionals from a very successful financial investment firm. I felt my mouth drop open and my self confidence wane as I watched my predecessor on stage . . . a gentleman whose animated and passionate talk about making money a priority included random shouts of "Profit! Profit! Profit!" with fists clenched and arms in the air. His enthusiasm alone ensured that his underlying message was clearly conveyed, and he certainly knew how to rile a crowd. I stood there wondering why I had been invited to share my message of living your dash, as it appeared to be in direct contrast with the primary theme and intended message of this conference. It was my first "paid gig" experience, and I felt as though I was preparing to jump into a lion's cage while covered in bacon. I feared that my message of slowing down, prioritizing, and realizing that making a life proves more important, ultimately, than making a living, would no doubt inflict emotional whiplash on this audience, and I was unnerved to the point of panic.

I had rehearsed my speech almost to memorization and had planned to conclude it with a heartfelt recitation of "The Dash" poem. However, for a brief moment, I was hesitant to share the message of "The Dash"—an ideal about which I'd always felt so strongly. Was I wrong to think that this life lesson could reach all spectrums of thought? Could sharing it at the wrong place at the wrong time prevent listeners from comprehending its true meaning? After all, I was asking them to consider expanding their hearts in lieu of their wallets. Would that have a rebound effect in these surroundings and ultimately demean my intent?

Somewhere in my awkward ascent up the stairs leading to the podium, I changed my plan in a moment of spontaneity. I decided to open with my ace in the hole. I stood at the podium and instead of thanking my emcee for his gracious introduction, I began reciting with deliberate emotion . . . "I read of a man who stood to speak . . . at the funeral of a friend." After I had read the last line of the poem, I took a slow, deep breath into my lungs and peered out into the eyes of several individuals in the front row. I instantly knew I had captured their attention. It was as if by speaking those thirty-six lines, I had unintentionally squelched the messages my predecessor had so power-fully left in his wake. It was as though the entire room experienced the same epiphany, simultaneously. Without further hesitation, I confidently contin-ued my speech and received a rousing standing ovation when it was over.

Afterward, I greeted many individuals at my book signing. One woman remarked that my presentation had begun to make her reevaluate her defini-tion of success. I smiled in return, as if to say: "Then, my work here is done."

Attaining success is wonderful. But, you must first honestly define or redefine your personal views of success. To do this, you need to identify and align your priorities. You, by yourself, through personal soul-searching, have to define what is (and what isn't) truly necessary for you to lead a satisfy-ing, fulfilling life. What is defined as a non-priority should be considered superfluous, and you should be okay with abandoning it without emotion. By definitively deciding what is necessary or unnecessary in your dash, you not only free yourself from the invisible chains of the excessive, but you train yourself to avoid the accumulation of additional needless items in the future.

Too often we are blinded by our ambition and cannot see the truth that most of what we are seeking in the form of material possessions is simply not what makes up the fabric of life. I've often used the following to illustrate the irony of our focus on tangible wealth: "You can't take it with you. Have you ever seen a hearse pulling a U-Haul?"

To help determine your definition of success, imagine your life as a con-glomerate. For illustrative purpose, let's call it "Me, Inc." How would you run your "business" most efficiently? Would you base its success on pure monetary net profit or would you balance profit and loss by comparing the value of what you've received to that which you've given back? If "Me, Inc." had to insure its most valued commodities, what would those be? If the warehouse went up in flames, what would you choose to salvage first?

So many people say money can't buy happiness. I understand that statement's intent, and perhaps its literal translation is true, but when you deal in real, you realize that money does have the unique ability to "buy" peace of mind. Peace of mind is the foundation upon which happiness is built. Optimistic poets, like myself, promote the belief that the good things in life are found, not in things, but in that which can never be replaced. However, the significance of money, and of financial well-being and stability, cannot be simply overlooked. Though a warm bed to sleep in, a roof over our heads, adequate medical care, and food on our tables are blessings we often take for granted, they are considered "riches" to many, because they do, in fact, require money. Therefore, indirectly, though it may sound callous and greedy—because it has the capability of bringing peace of mind—money can, indirectly, buy happiness.

Yet, money is a double-edged sword. Though it can provide peace of mind, it can just as easily be the catalyst that prevents you from gaining that peace. I'd venture to say it is the most time-consuming, stress-inducing facet of our lives. We invest hours dreaming about it, desiring it, seeking various avenues from which to attain it, deciding how best to spend it, following it, and counting it. However, the most prevalent peace-sucking attribute of money is when desire overcomes practicality, and we find ourselves in debt. This creates a multitude of stress inducers that can easily become direly "debtrimental" to our health and well-being. I've created an acronym for debt to remind myself not to reach for that colorful, efficient, three-inch plastic card that lives and thrives in my wallet: **D.E.B.T.—Don't Even Be There.**

How do you recognize when you're deeper in debt than you should be? When you borrow from Peter to pay Paul and then the following month, borrow from Paul to pay Peter back what you borrowed from him to pay Paul. The first time this scenario occurs, it should be considered a red flag indicating a destructive sequence.

Debt is a powerful detour on the road toward emotional well-being and peace of mind. Banks and financial institutions adorn it in seductive, ornate packages in attempts to divert our focus away from fine print, deadlines, penalties, and annual fees. Then, they name their elaborate creations: CREDIT. They lure us in by capitalizing on our weakest attribute: desire. They pursue our desire until we are ensnared in a trap like a wounded wildebeest in the jaws of a hungry lion. Put succinctly, committing your future to pay for your past is a quick and easy way to destroy life's tranquility.

We've all been witness to the power of money. The weighty influence it has on the world is exemplified in a range of hackneyed clichés, from "Money makes the world go 'round" to "Money is the root of all evil"—both of which are 100 percent accurate.

Live Your Dash.

How Much Do You Make an Hour?

"Daddy, how much do you make an hour?"
the boy asked inquisitively.
His father glanced at him and said,
"I'm busy now . . . don't bother me."

"But daddy, I'd really like to know
how much do you get paid?
Please tell me after you've worked one hour,
how much money have you made?"

His father's face formed an expression
as though receiving an insult
and said, "That's not the type of question
you should ask of an adult!

Such an inquiry is rude
and to you, it really shouldn't matter.
Now go along and play;
I don't have time for idle chatter!"

The father sat to read his report,
but as he turned each page . . .
he wondered why his son was curious
about his hourly wage?

He called the boy to return
and said, "Son, before you go . . .
I earn twenty dollars an hour.
Now, tell me why you want to know."

The father sat beside him
loosening the tie around his collar
and his son asked, "If that's how much,
may I borrow just ten dollars?

I'll pay it back with my allowance.
I promise that I will!"
And curious of his son's intent,
he reached for a ten-dollar bill.

The boy ran into his bedroom
and gave his mattress a quick lift,
then reached to grab a ten-dollar bill
he'd received as a birthday gift.

He handed his father the money—
"Daddy, I know your time's not free,
but now I can give you twenty dollars
to spend one hour just with me!"

Nice Things

Things: Like falling snow, they accumulate everywhere. They can slowly steal our freedom and clutter our reality. They weigh like anchors upon our clarity of mind. They infect simplicity by using chaos and confusion. They cloud otherwise transparent views of life's beauty. They cause a misalignment in priorities.

Many people believe "things" make them happy. This may be true for some, but it is a fleeting joy that dissipates after the new wears off. As our possessions grow, they limit our ability to travel lightly upon the earth. We slowly allow them to begin representing an importance in our lives, albeit a hollow, counterfeit importance. We begin to consider them as outward decorations of ourselves—proclamations of our successes.

I was meandering around the home furnishings section of a local department store one day when I overheard one woman say to another, "Oh, I'm going to pick this up for Eleanor . . . she has such nice things!" I could feel a sarcastic smirk appear across my face as I began to imagine what qualities a "thing" might possess in order for it to be described as "nice." I envisioned Eleanor's nice things smiling cordially at one another on the mantle. I visualized her nice knickknacks exchanging courteous comments from their temporary residences on the coffee table. I imagined overhearing the compliments her nice things bestowed upon each other from within the drawers of her jewelry box. I wondered if her nice dinner candles said "pardon me" to the nice candlesticks when their wax overflowed or if her nice lamps used "please" and "thank you" when requesting new bulbs.

I briefly recalled the scene from *Beauty and the Beast* in which the candelabra, Lumiere, the pendulum clock, Cogsworth, and Mrs. Potts, the kindhearted teapot, danced merrily around the room with the other "nice" things that resided in the castle. I thought how Eleanor's friends and family must admire the manners she had instilled into these items since purchasing them and bringing them home. After all, they were all so nice.

Among a slew of synonyms listed under the word *nice*, I found: *courteous, amiable, pleasant, kind,* and *polite.* I paused to ask myself at what point did it become possible that a tangible, nonliving organism could aptly be described using any of these words? *Attractive?* Yes. *Shiny?* Sure. *Appealing?* Uh huh. But, *nice?* Not so much.

I believe that point stems from our obsession with possessions, which I assert began right around the time we started referring to objects, belongings, and even vehicles as "nice." At that time, we allowed them to cross over an invisible boundary. Things and stuff began to enter our lives as something more . . . something we would attach our emotions to, thereby escalating their value to that which was more than merely monetary.

Maybe "they" did this intentionally! Maybe "they" are in cahoots with the insurance companies in a "Desire to Acquire" conspiracy! After all, the more we own, the more we must insure, right? Perhaps, if these items indeed have the ability to be nice, they might very well possess the capabilities to be cunning and conniving, as well!

Let's face it: the word *nice*, when used in this fashion can most often be substituted with either of the words *costly* or *valuable.* "Nice things" is but a convenient phrase used instead of saying something like: "Eleanor has spent a good deal of her money on her possessions . . ." It is a phrase for which the honest intent translates into: items of monetary value.

"She lives in a nice home." "She drives a nice car." "She has nice things." All of these statements truly mean that Eleanor is pretty well-off financially. After all, her home could be downright obstinate, her car might interrupt conversations and belch in public, and her possessions could be offensive and ill mannered, but if they were pricey and can be envied by friends and neighbors, they are usually called "nice" regardless.

Furthermore, I've often found it curious that people refer to a tangible item as "holding" memories. Really? Where? Memories aren't held by any particular object. They are held in our minds. They are held in our hearts. We alone keep them safe. We alone bring them to the forefront and relive them at will. We alone "hold" them. Granted, a specific object from our past might spark recollections of bygone days, but things are things. They are constructed from disposable materials. They have no feelings. They have no heart. They are not nice. Grandma's vase and Aunt Felicia's chipped china plates are things. They once served their purpose in someone's life, yet we tend to treasure and cherish them as if they have literally recreated within themselves, the aura, attributes and qualities of their previous owners.

If you were to choose the top ten blessings that are present in your life right now, what would you choose? For argument's sake, let's say that these ten items are the only possessions you'll be able to keep in your life from this point forward. Hopefully, not many things made it to your list, if any . . . not even the "nice" ones.

I used to work with a woman who, though reasonably kind and considerate, placed far too much emphasis on physical belongings. It seemed to most everyone who knew her for more than thirty minutes that her main objective in life was to constantly acquire more: more expensive cars, bigger houses, better jewelry. She truly found what I considered to be a distorted happiness in her acquisitions and possessions. When someone in the office had a birthday or anniversary approaching and planned to celebrate that evening, upon their return to the office the next morning, she would immediately approach, hurling her familiar inquiry: "What'd ya get?" After awhile, it became a catch phrase used around the office to mock her materialism. It became a routine that after President's Day, Labor Day, New Year's, or Boxing Day in Canada, we would jokingly ask each other, "What'd ya get?"

I don't think there is anything particularly wrong with partially equating success with that which we purchase, own, and appreciate. It is a good feeling to have and enjoy the extra amenities hard work may afford us. It is all about how much emphasis we place on the value of these items and the percentage we believe their ownership contributes to our happiness. I maintain the belief that what should be considered most precious and what is truly invaluable in our lives is that which we cannot purchase. "The best things in life are free" is one of the most overused, yet sincere, morally correct clichés ever spoken. I read the following statement on a bumper sticker years ago, and it has remained on my mind, since: "Measure wealth not by what you have, but by what you have and would not sell." This theory would make us all millionaires.

If you have a constant desire to acquire more than you require, ask yourself, why? Is it to validate yourself by using purchases to exhibit to others that you have become a successful individual? Is it to bring attention to yourself? Is it to satisfy an unidentified void in your life? Do you truly believe that obtaining more things brings you happiness? Is it greed? When does it stop? Do you find yourself in the destructive, insatiable cycle of acquiring more things only to discover you want more things? Shopping, buying, owning—a three-step process whose ultimate result is nothing more than shallow transient, satisfaction. Familiarity may breed contempt, but it also breeds dissatisfaction. We become used to things rather quickly and, therefore, want to experience the "new" again. It is only when we are able to recognize and clearly foresee the inevitable familiarity downfall that we can break our addiction to the "new."

I'm reminded of the saying, "He who dies with the most toys wins . . . " The time we have on Earth is precious. Things aren't. The love we share is invaluable. Things aren't. The laughter we exchange is spontaneous. Things aren't. What we leave behind in the hearts and minds of others is that by which we are truly remembered. Things aren't. Life is nice. Things aren't.

Structure/Stricture

Structure: a system or organization made up of interrelated parts functioning as a whole. **Stricture:** a limit or restriction, especially one that seems unfair or too harsh.

I am a wordsmith. Automatically when I read words, my mind connects them . . . thinking of similarities, links to other words, and oddities they may contain. A good example of this played out over a weekend that my husband and I spent in the country. We stayed at a hotel nestled in the hills of a small town in east Tennessee where the view from our window consisted of a large field of cows. I had made a commitment to write some stories while visiting this tranquil environment and found myself staring out the window at the beauty of the mountains and the trees . . . and the cows. Admittedly, I'd never spent much of my time wondering about cows, but as I watched them, at least peripherally, for hours, I became more curious about their habits and behaviors. I watched them eat. And eat. And eat. I noticed how neatly manicured the grounds were on this acreage and realized it was due, in large part, not to endless hours of this Tennessee farmer's sweat and toil, but to a bovine intervention. *Ingenious*, I thought, as I vowed solemnly that if, by some strange turn of events, I was ever bequeathed acreage, I would be a proud cow owner. My point is, when I'd put together the sight of the beautiful grounds of this estate, and the reasons behind it, my mind instantly exchanged one letter in cow to form the word mow. This is a simple example of how the gears of a wordsmith's mind work . . .

Using the same letter replacement exercise, I recently noted the similarities of the words *structure* and *stricture*. As I began to write this book, I slowly convinced myself that it had to have a solid structure. For years, I had been a freelance writer, penning anything and everything. Very few stories and poems I'd written were connected, with the exception of the obvious shared theme: life. However, I felt that writing a book with numbered pages and linked stories would require a more consistent flow and definite cohesion to be most effective for the reader. It was though a wild mare had been suddenly put in the barn. For weeks, the creative flow was stifled in my mind. Ideas were everywhere, but how could I make the stories "fit" together into one book?

I had created time lines, chapter titles, and strategies. I'd printed bold acronyms, word maps, and index cards until my office walls began to resemble a strategic military operational headquarters. There were arrows, sticky notes, and bullet points in every direction. Yet with all of this structure, the words of the stories failed to flow. I felt as though I had a marathon to run, but my legs were deeply embedded in a pit of thick quick sand.

Then a lesson came to mind that I'd learned from a group at an assisted-living facility at which I once began conducting a weekly writing class. Those who had opted to join were interested in writing about their "dashes," their lives, in order to leave something valuable and tangible for their loved ones someday. Initially, we had about a dozen or so members, and as time went on, the membership grew.

During our first meeting, I'd expressed the meaning and sentiment behind "The Dash," followed by sharing an emotional recitation of the poem to receptive ears. It seemed, at the time, that the enthusiasm in their reactions was overflowing. I was also anxious to receive and read their stories, as recollected by each of them, about the people and places they'd encountered in their many years. After all, I'd roughly calculated while focusing briefly, clockwise from eye to eye, that there were at least nine hundred combined years of life's experiences, right there in the room with me. I'd left that day with a positive feeling, as if my efforts were going to make a difference in some lives.

Upon my arrival for the second meeting, however, I was rather disappointed to receive only one story from a member in the group. I thought

I must have somehow misread their initial zeal for the project. I began a discussion with the thought in the back of my mind that maybe this writing group wasn't as wonderful an idea as I had believed.

Then they began to share, one by one, that they had started to write but feared they had forgotten the proper grammar rules, punctuation, verb tenses, etc. Some said they had written stories, but were later embarrassed to share them because they weren't "perfect." A few had even excitedly exchanged written stories with each other, only to have them returned with red X's and circles, much like a teacher's critique from grade school. They had anticipated I would be doing the same. Though their stories and memories flowed like Niagara Falls verbally, when they began to put sentences to paper, they were inhibited by the semicolon, prepositional phrase, and dangling participle rules of their past. Because they felt I expected structure, there was stricture.

I realized I should have expressed to them that I was not a teacher, nor an instructor (a.k.a. "in-structure") of any kind, and that the story itself was the main target, not the use of correct punctuation and proper verbiage. I encouraged them to focus not on the complex rules that had been ingrained in their minds from English class but instead on the words, the memories, the places, and the faces.

The next week I was pleasantly surprised by creative, wonderful stories filled with memories, hopes, and dreams that they had written purposely for the benefit of their friends and families.

One gentleman, in particular, wrote a story that stays with me to this day. He had likened his own life to that of a locomotive. The train he had referenced kept moving rapidly forward, never in reverse. The train took on new passengers and would stop to let others off. He compared the arriving passengers to those friendships and relationships he had established along the way, and the passengers who stepped off the train represented both casual acquaintances and loved ones he had lost. It was an amazing story, and I wish to this day I had made a copy. But I guess the memory and the life lesson his story inspired within me were all that was meant to be.

I began to understand that as soon as I removed the structure they had assumed I would require from their stories, the stricture was removed, as well. They were free to let their minds wander, remember, and thus record recollections of times they had spent, both the good and the bad. The results were gratifying to me—and to them—and the project continued after I left.

I recalled that life lesson when I opened my own mind to freely write this book. I will continue writing without structure, about life, because that is how life is offered. I know that when the stories for the book are finished, a coherent circle will bind them, because they will have been created from the most important single commonality we share—life. True creativity contains no structure, no stricture.

Do you have so much structure in your life, that it creates stricture? Do current obligations, responsibilities, and deadlines prevent you from tapping into your own creative mind? What changes can you make in your life, either physically or mentally, to free yourself from the chains of structure/stricture and experience instantaneous release and relief?

Adaptation

A beautiful dogwood tree once graced our front yard. It lived and thrived well, offering its perfect four-petal blooms for more than ten seasons, without fail. It was a wonderful addition to our landscaping, having spent its entire existence residing under the shade and protection of a thirty-year-old pine tree. Unfortunately, the large pine grew sick and began randomly losing heavy limbs in dangerous fashion. We reluctantly had it removed from the yard. The gentleman who cut it down went to great lengths, involving ropes and calculated angles, in a valiant, painstaking attempt to save the fragile dogwood tree. Afterward, we all believed he had succeeded, because the beloved dogwood tree appeared to be unharmed and stood as proud and beautiful as ever.

After the pine was cut down and removed, the days passed, and the sun shone mercilessly upon the branches and delicate blooms of the dogwood. Our tree was being forced to endure the harsh reality of nature as it never had before. No longer was there a large tree filtering the sun and offering protection from the unforgiving wind and the weather. No longer was there a guardian neighbor shielding the tree from life's hardships, like a parent or devoted friend. Daily, I watched as it tried desperately to survive in its new circumstances. Though I tried to assist it in its struggles, painstakingly following advice from a local horticulturist, I witnessed the slow demise of this embodiment of nature's wonder. The tree simply could not adapt to the additional sunshine, precipitation, and change in its surroundings. Alas, our tree could not proceed, succeed, and survive.

Most of us have heard the originally untitled Serenity Prayer, which is now attributed to the theologian Reinhold Niebuhr: "God, grant me the serenity to accept the things I cannot change; courage to change the things I can; and wisdom to know the difference."

Far be it for me to challenge this time-tested mantra to millions. However, I believe the first two aspects of this beloved message should be reversed. If you believe in, and wish to practice, the intention of this beautiful insight, wouldn't you first and foremost request the courage to change the things you can before requesting the serenity to accept that which you cannot? Otherwise, how would you know? How can you accept what you cannot change if you first don't try to change it? Praying for the courage to change the things you can, in my opinion, should precede accepting that which you cannot. Recognize. Implement. Proceed.

Adaptation undoubtedly leads to reaching a higher level on the satisfaction meter of life. Adaptation involves both a willingness to change and evolve, and/or recognize, accept, and adapt to that which we are powerless to change.

I recently read about a particular breed of penguin that is naturally considered by most to be a cold-water species. These penguins, living by the equator year-round, have ingeniously adapted to their surroundings in an attempt to increase the survival and success of future generations. (Or one might argue, to increase opportunities to live their dash!) Unlike their Antarctic counterparts that have succumbed to accepting what they cannot change and risking their lives by facing the hazards of freezing temperatures in order to incubate their eggs and potential offspring, the penguins found near the Galapagos Islands rely on a brilliant adaptation: they deposit their eggs in safe, shady areas and crevices of the warm volcanic rock, allowing nature to do the work for them. Approximately five weeks later—little penguins!

Adapting to any shift in your norm requires stepping past the boundaries of your self-created "comfort zone," whether voluntarily or involuntarily. This action will ultimately result in a life experience—be the end result positive or negative. Every life experience we undergo, the good and the bad, melds into the very crux of who we are today and who we become tomorrow.

History has proven time and again that those who adapt well to change, those who honestly consider suggestions and ideas for improvement though it may mean swallowing their pride at times, and those who welcome such changes, have a better chance at achieving success in life, than those who oppose. Compare an unrelenting, steadfast hardwood tree to the bending, flexible, adaptable willow. The solid unremitting trunk of a hardwood represents strength, power, and fortitude, while the weeping willow evokes quite the opposite image. Yet, in the willow's apparent weakness is found its greatest strength—the ability to adapt, and thus survive and thrive. In essence, its instability also enables its adaptability.

I often compare two groups of opposite personality traits to the hardwood and the willow trees. The hardwood group comprises those who oppose—those who oppose change, suggestions, new ideas, and plans in any form. Their opposition is usually presented immediately and often spontaneously out of habit. Sometimes the opposer will defend or debate a moot issue for the sheer sake of argument. They switch into "defense attorney" mode and will argue that sea levels are reduced by the amount of water left on a surfer emerging from the waves. Though it is indeed fact, it is also completely irrelevant. Facts are usually the first casualty in any battle of words in which they find themselves. If this group had a symbol to represent them, it would be a statue of an individual standing stern, arms folded tightly around his chest, creating a formidable barrier between him and any and all changes looming on the horizon. Individuals in the hardwood group instantly view alterations or modifications to what they have become accustomed to in their comfort zone as foreign or unnecessary. Hardwoods are, therefore, reluctant to attempt to put change into practice, often labeling it "wrong" from the outset. Members of this group view life through their "if it's not broken, don't fix it" bifocals.

The willow group comprises those who understand, welcome, and easily adapt to life's continually changing climate. If this group were to have an icon to represent its core existence, it would be that of a child, for a child's heart and mind are untarnished and alive with a fresh innocence that welcomes change, challenges, and choices. Individuals in the willow group do not curse the weather but rather rejoice in the beauty of what follows the rain. Eventually however, both the hardwood and the willow have to face the powerful and merciless wind.

When the winds of change blow strong and hard and adjustments are inevitable, the willow group bends and sways like the willow tree, relinquishing its stance to the ever-changing direction of these powerful forces. The willow relies on its perceived weakness as its greatest strength and, therefore, survives each of life's unpredictable storms, emerging bent but not broken, stripped of branches and leaves, but content in the belief in its ability to grow back stronger, greener, and fuller than before. Standing as proud as it always had, it will once again be receptive to new experiences and new perspectives, and be ready to encounter more of the inevitable constant: change.

The hardwood, on the other hand, fights the winds of life's storms until it can fight no longer. It remains staunch and unyielding, fruitlessly challenging positive, progressive currents of change and compromise until either it is forced, unwillingly, to surrender, or its stubborn limbs and trunk splinter and fracture as the two collide. The hardwood group's own determined, willful negativity could ultimately lead to downfall. And if, by chance, it survives the clash seemingly unharmed, it remains the same—uninspired, unchanged, unyielding, and undeviating in its position. The willow gives change a chance. The hardwood will not chance a change.

I am not suggesting it is healthy practice to consistently compromise your core beliefs or convictions. Instead, I urge you to remain open-minded and to readily accept new and different ideas, concepts and modes of operating. I do not believe that every change is always for the better. However, in making your decision, consider that the farther you step away from the boundaries of the comfort zone that protects you, the more you can learn, the more you can experience what life has to offer, and the more you are able to fully live your dash! When the winds of change blow strong in your direction, sway, bow, and flow willingly in the direction of their gusts. You will survive and emerge stronger, wiser, and more experienced. However, if you instead continue insisting on resisting, through inflexibility or plain obstinacy, you may break or remain virtually stagnant like the hardwood. Listening, compromising, and sometimes yielding to what you may not always perceive as the right of way, are all components of adaptability and imperative if you are to grow, learn, develop, and enhance your dash.

Are you a hardwood or a willow?

WHEN LIFE'S JOURNEY PRESENTS DETOURS

AND ROUTES CHANGE WITH EVERY MILE,

REMEMBER A ROAD THAT HAS NO OBSTACLES

LEADS NOWHERE WORTHWHILE . . .

Passion (Find Yours)

It's been said that the key to happiness is to find something you love doing and then discover a way to make a living doing it. What if what you love is weaving baskets from banana peels or designing crafts from pomegranate seeds? Of course, I'm being facetious, but some passions obviously won't make lucrative professions, no matter how much you wishfully finagle market fluctuations or supply and demand. I find it interesting that the word *vocation* has become synonymous with the words *career, job,* and *profession.* The word *vocation* itself is derived from the Latin meaning: "to call." It is a blessed few who can say that their career today—their job—is their calling.

Many who dole out advice strictly to inspire others are not being realistic when they say, "You can make a career out of anything you are passionate about!" Maybe that statement was true fifty years ago, but the consumer today is far more selective, having far more options from which to choose. As a person who is actually making a living using her passion (writing), I can honestly say it is certainly a major contributor to peace and fulfillment in life. However, before I discovered ways to derive my income from it, I did it purely because I love it.

There are many success stories from people who have taken passions such as skateboarding or growing herbs and turned them into full-time, profitable careers. By all means, while being honest and realistic, if you see avenues from which to derive an income using the talents and skills of your true passion, then follow your heart in that direction. I am a firm believer in Norman Vincent Peale's quote: "Throw your heart over the fence and the rest will follow." However, if the market dictates otherwise or fear of losing stability prevents you from taking that leap of faith, do not abandon your passion! If you feel you cannot make a living from your passion, you can still make a life with it. Find ways to weave it into the fabric of your life. It can still be the fuel that lights your fire, which you carry with you in your mind and soul and which helps give your presence purpose.

How do you discover your passion, what it is you feel you were meant to do, if it's not immediately evident to you?

Follow different ideas. Try before you buy. You carry seeds of greatness within you—how do you know which ones will thrive if you don't cultivate and nourish each one of them? Give them a chance to develop and grow.

- What makes you enthusiastic when you think or talk about it?

- What signs have you received indicating your special talents or interests are greater than average?

- What do you do with particular ease and enjoyment?

- What is it that makes the thrill of challenge greater than the fear of failure?

INTERNAL CLOCK

We all have individual biological clocks that give our bodies signs when it is most beneficial for us to sleep and to rise. These are incredible timepieces: invisible, waterproof, and self-winding! Unfortunately, for many of us, our chosen vocations and careers do not run parallel with our internal time clock. In order to function efficiently, we often are forced to adapt our inner rhythms to sync with the world's time clock. Though alarm clocks and specific times for events, such as breakfast, lunch, and dinner, are in direct contradiction with what we feel inside, we allow them to dictate our actions.

I have despised waking early since as far back as I can remember. Whenever I was forced to rise early for school or work, my body parts would unite and execute a mutiny against me. Society made it impossible for me to dance to my own internal rhythm, perform at my own pace, and follow the minutes and hours of my internal timepiece, all because school started at 8:00 a.m.

My mantra was, "It may be the early bird who catches the worm, but it's the second mouse who gets the cheese . . ." And as I advanced into adulthood, the situation worsened. Everyone, it appeared, believed in the early worm approach, and I realized being the second mouse wasn't going to get me anywhere in the corporate world. So, I made adjustments. Since I was unable to adjust my job to my clock, I adjusted my clock to my job. Although doing so made me more efficient and productive, I never felt the balance. I was close but still off-kilter. I felt like a radio dial set to 98.3, when the strong station signals came from 98.5.

Let's face it—early in life, we are denied the choice to discover and follow our internal time clocks. We are taught when to wake, when to eat, and when to sleep. If we were fortunate enough to recognize the workings of our individual timepieces in time to align them to our vocation instead of society's rules, the result would be an equation for true success. The gears of the world are linked in such a way that we, in order to form a more perfect union, must flow in the direction of their rotations. However, the gears that are in operation during daylight hours seem to be the most productive. Night owls and those of us who despise the abbreviation "a.m." when a number from six to eight precedes it, are many times those who must reset our internal clocks and adjust our timing.

WHO YOU ARE

I'd experienced an interesting insight while having lunch one day with a gentleman from my previous life in the corporate world. Prior to accepting the position that made him my boss, Colonel Kleimon was a decorated officer in the U.S. armed forces. Though hesitant to speak freely or answer questions about his emotional encounters during the wars in which he had proudly served his country, I did manage to draw an answer out of him that made a profound impact on me in the years that followed. I asked him, why—why he, and why they, do what they do. Obviously it hadn't been for the accolades, as his medals of valor and awarded honors were tucked into drawers and rarely, if ever, spoken of—they certainly weren't hung on the wall to beckon praise. Indeed, it wasn't for the money, as the physical investment, the risks, and the dangers obviously far outweigh the income potential. He answered with four simple words: "It's Who You Are."

I asked myself immediately if what I was doing with my life represented who I was. I further probed my mind to ask if who I actually was that day reflected who I was supposed to be. To find the answers to those questions, I had to peel back the layers of life's minutiae to reach the core of me. Not the me I had let life in the twenty-first century become, but the me I was meant to be. I had to dig deep and search my soul to finally discover that the answer was *no*.

My line of work in the corporate world didn't follow the path of my ideals or my beliefs, and certainly did not reflect the Colonel's principle of "It's Who You Are." Yet, I had to earn a paycheck. In order to fill what I believed was a large, gaping hole, I had to add more of myself, the real me, into my daily life. Although I continued to focus on my job, I found creative ways to fuse the tasks that made my heart content, ways that were more like Who I Am, into my days. By doing so, I discovered a balance. I succeeded in steadying the continuous rocking of the boat of discontent I had been feeling inside.

Does what you do represent who you are? If not, find ways to bring enough of yourself and your values to your current position in life to create that missing fulfillment. Look externally, outside the comfort zone of your employment if necessary, to find ways to bring yourself closer to who you are.

Invisible Fences

As I walked with a friend through my neighborhood one afternoon, a fierce, angry dog charged out of the bushes as we passed his home, the territory he literally lives to defend and protect. Startled, I jumped back, but then I watched as he stopped mid-stride, stood momentarily motionless, and then turned to walk back toward the front porch. I realized that his owners had installed an "invisible fence." It is invisible because the fence relies on buried cable, which connects wirelessly to the dog's collar. When the dog, wearing this collar, crosses the boundary area, he receives a mild electric shock. My furry foe had reached the boundary of his safe zone that day, and his acquired reflexive action made him cease and desist.

Although I don't encourage or condone this type of animal training, I couldn't ignore the correlation between invisible fences and the boundaries in our own lives (with the exception, fortunately, of electric shock!). Many of us have subconsciously installed invisible fences—the unseen obstacles that prevent us from venturing beyond our safety zones and toward our dreams, hopes, and goals. You may encounter many different types of invisible fences. However, they all have one thing in common: YOU. They were installed only by you and can be removed only by you.

SELF-BOUT

Every goal you reach on the way to success is attained through a struggle, an internal battle, a fight between two wills. The two adversaries of this match-up are on opposite sides of the ring in every way. The first opponent will seize every opportunity for immediate gratification, even if it results in the sacrifice or postponement of an aspiration. The challenger realizes that to obtain a goal, one must sometimes forfeit instant indulgences and that in order to remain focused on the target, distractions must appear only in peripheral vision. Striving for success will create this internal struggle often. It is a fight—a fight between self-gratitude and self-discipline—a self-bout.

The best way I've found to ensure self-discipline is for the victor to follow Thomas Huxley's advice: "Do what you should do, when you should do it, whether you feel like it or not." Self-discipline is a combination of willpower and persistence. Willpower to resist the temptations offered by self-gratification and the persistence to continue resisting until a goal is achieved. Having self-discipline means you have the ability to begin an action, regardless of the state of your current emotions. Self-discipline is a fundamental and vital tool in eliminating procrastination and disorder.

Building and maintaining self-discipline is made more difficult because it takes self-discipline to begin using self-discipline. It's the chicken and the egg question—which comes first? Self-discipline must be strengthened and utilized in order to become most effective, and it is strengthened best through challenges. The more challenges you face and conquer, the stronger and more confident you become. You have to learn to literally confront yourself to win each self-bout. As soon as excuses start to enter your mind, build a wall to stop them. Repeat the three words to yourself: JUST DO IT. You will soon discover that the more disciplined you become, the easier your life will be.

IMPATIENCE

Instant gratification has become commonplace in the slice-and-bake mentality of the twenty-first century. With high-speed Internet access and overnight web mogul millionaires, it is easy to begin to expect immediate results. In fact, we have become so accustomed to the immediate fulfillment of our desires that we are inclined to give up if we don't receive the results we are seeking as soon as we had expected or anticipated. We always have to remember that everything worthwhile is worth waiting for. Reaching a well-established goal is probably not something that will happen overnight. If you're not willing to invest the time and effort, perhaps consider a particular challenge simply a task to add to your to-do list, instead of labeling it a "goal."

FEAR OF FAILURE

People may fear failure, but the fear of its consequences can prove to be even greater. The fear-of-failure factor can be incapacitating and a huge hindrance in progression toward a dream or goal. It is not a single entity, but comprises many sub-fears, such as the fear of rejection and fear of criticism. Successful people are successful because they have determined early in life's journey that failure breeds success. They have learned to embrace their blunders and accept them for what they are: lessons in disguise.

Dr. Robert Schuller wrote one of the most challenging and introspective questions I've ever read in his book, *If It's Going to Be, It's up to Me: The Eight Proven Principles of Possibility Thinking*: "What would you do if you knew you could not fail?" After considering his inquiry, the possibilities running through my mind were endless. I began using the word *perhaps* more often. Using the word *perhaps* frequently in conversations with yourself invites positive beliefs and action. If you've become comfortable with an "easier said than done" attitude, maybe you're right, but how will you know until you try?

Do your ideas, goals, and aspirations fall under the "It looks good on paper, but will it run?" scenario? We invest so much of our time and effort in the scheming and planning phases that preparation itself proves to be an invisible fence. When we're afraid of potential devastation from potential disappoint from potential failure, we limit potential success. Who are the people you feel you may disappoint if it doesn't "run"? If the person on the top of the list is you, get over it! Initiate action. To overcome the fear factor, convert your planning steps into action steps and take the first one. Visions and good intentions alone do not initiate action. Many people plan and scrutinize details in preparation of a plan but fail to follow through. Like devoted architects, they scheme, draw, and connect the dots by creating elaborate blueprints but never get around to building the house.

Too much advice we read applies to the middle part of a project, in which your initial enthusiasm and energy has fizzled, and you are trudging toward the finish line. However the beginning, especially when you're looking at the daunting task of creating major changes in your life, can be disheartening, as well. The first step is the steepest.

Consider this scenario: If six birds are sitting on a telephone wire and one makes the decision to fly away, how many birds are now on the wire? The answer is not five, as one might assume. The answer is six. One bird decided to fly away, but the thought itself did not remove him from the wire or change his current circumstances. A thought is a mere premeditation. A step is a physical action. Are you like this bird? Do you continually "decide" to make positive changes in your dash, but never take steps to turn your decisions into actions? Avoid too much analyzing, and take physical steps toward your goals. You can read a thermometer, but the only way to find out how cold the water feels is to get your feet wet.

Less than Perfect

For many, the fear of taking that first step occurs because in their minds, they cannot envision a successful outcome as anything less than a resounding success. They are hesitant to invest time and effort toward a goal because they are afraid the product won't shine above all others.

For perfectionists, good enough just isn't good enough and simply trying is not a consideration. Seeing a project through to perfect completion is the only option they will consider. Some feel that refusing to begin a new venture is better than having their efforts result in a less-than-perfect outcome. Therefore, doing and accomplishing nothing is more acceptable to them than achieving that which is not exceptional.

Those who seek perfection dictate unrealistic and often unattainable goals accompanied by persistent, self-defeating thoughts. They don't realize that accepting nothing less than perfection denies them the opportunity and experience to do something for the sake of just doing it. They are cheating themselves out of the enjoyment of the process itself in believing that the value is found only in sheer accomplishment.

An invisible fence of perfectionism is based on fear of the occasional blunder, miscalculation, or error. Perfectionists devote their time and energy around the clock to avoiding those, and when they inevitably do occur, perfectionists spend days reliving and regretting them. They view their human imperfections as deficiencies and flaws. To them, to err is to expose a vulnerability, a weak link in the chain of perfection for which they strive. They avoid criticism and disapproval by attempting all—or nothing. You don't need to be perfect to be excellent!

SET GOALS BASED ON YOUR SKILLS AND IDEALS—

WHAT YOU'VE DREAMED, HOPED, AND BELIEVED,

FOR IF YOUR ONLY DIRECTION

POINTS TOWARD REACHING PERFECTION,

YOUR GOALS WILL BE SELDOM ACHIEVED.

QTIP (QUIT TAKING IT PERSONALLY)

Failure is a result, an outcome. Failure is not a trait. If you begin to believe otherwise, you are simply being oversensitive. Those who display the weakness of oversensitivity can only attribute (or blame) this undue personality flaw on learned behavior, not to an innate or a hereditary characteristic. Though their unique experiences of disappointment and the presence of others' consistent pessimistic behavior are major contributors, the culprit for the development of this character imperfection is their own reactions to those contributors. The first time someone takes rejection or refusal personally, it plants a seed . . . one that grows exponentially, cultivated each time it receives more negative feedback or criticism.

Our response to negative comments and opinions directly determines their impact. If someone says no to a request or disapproves of your idea or project, that person is not always rejecting you. If you feel hurt or rejected, it may have something to do with how you feel about yourself. If you twist, mangle, or (purposefully?) misconstrue even the most well-meaning actions, you need to remember to QTIP—Quit Taking It Personally! When you stop feeling like the victim, you can begin to see the positive aspects and opportunities behind every rejection, refusal, or denial. You begin to see rejection as, simply, redirection.

Additionally, in this day of lightning-speed communication, the potential for misconstruing written words that appear on a phone or computer screen and therefore lack the intended voice inflection, is high. Therefore, the benefit of the doubt should always be granted, and a QTIP approach applied. A great example of this is a faux pas committed innocently by my oldest brother. A novice to the world of instant technological communication, he had met a woman who apparently was quite the opposite. In a vain attempt to compliment the speed at which she had sent text replies to him, he tried to impress her by matching her rapid typing skills. His awkward fingers omitted the "s" from the word "fast." He quickly sent a text back to her, intending it as a compliment: "You're SO fat!" Fortunately for him, she followed a QTIP strategy, and the relationship continued.

COMFORT ZONE

Your comfort zone is a plot of mental acreage enclosed within imaginary boundaries you have created. It houses the familiar, the recognizable, the unchallenged, the predictable, the banal . . . along with a perceived security resulting from all of these. Living your life primarily within "the zone" is inarguably one of the most difficult invisible fences to hurdle. The security of an unrewarding job, the predictability of an unfulfilling relationship, the instant self-gratification of a bad habit, the friendship based solely on proximity or familiarity, the relationship built and sustained primarily due to loneliness: all pillars of unhappiness that will stand until you relinquish the security you find in your comfort zone.

A television show in the early sixties often began with these words: "There is a fifth dimension beyond that which is known to man. It is a dimension as vast as space and as timeless as infinity. It is the middle ground between light and shadow, between science and superstition, and it lies between the pit of man's fears and the summit of his knowledge. This is the dimension of imagination. It is an area which we call 'The Twilight Zone.'"

Sarcastically, I ask the rhetorical question: On some level are you afraid that stepping beyond the comfort zone might place you into another dimension, from which you will be unable to return? What are the negative aspects of stepping beyond your safe boundaries? When you thoughtfully consider the pros versus the cons of exploring new opportunities, taking emotional risks, and living your dash, you'll find that the pros far outweigh the cons. In other words, realistically, what have you got to lose by trying?

It's important to remember to venture out of your comfort zone at your own pace, so you won't be discouraged in the process. Consider these two types of people going swimming in a pool when the water is cold: The first will place only his feet in the water, then slowly ease his body in, inches at a time, allowing it to slowly become accustomed to the change in temperature. The second, without hesitation, jumps into the middle of the cold pool. The ultimate goal of the two individuals is the same, yet the methods they use to achieve it are quite opposite. They know what works best for them, individually.

SOMEDAY SYNDROME

Have you added an extra day to your vocabulary: Friday, Saturday, Sunday . . . Someday? Do most of the sentences from conversations you share about your dreams and aspirations begin with the words *if* and *when*?

When I lose weight . . . If I get that promotion . . . When I retire . . . If things change . . . When my luck get better . . . When I get organized . . . When my life turns around . . .

Today was the last day of someone's dash . . . somewhere. Do you think his or her Someday ever came? Someday never comes for many. On that note, Sunday may never come for many; 6:00 p.m. tomorrow may never come for many. Are you merely existing and waking up each day to follow the same motions from the day before? Are you sleepwalking through life and postponing happiness until a self-created "if" or "when" event happens?

It is great to set goals and to focus your mindset on meeting those goals, but to actually mentally postpone true satisfaction in your life pending the attainment of your goals does not figure into any true "happiness equation." Days go by whether you are close to achieving or have made strides toward reaching your self-made happiness goals or not. Days go by. It's been said that happiness is a journey, not a destination. Using that philosophy, we should strive to be happy, satisfied, and content on the way to reaching our goals, not putting off true happiness and contentment until we get there, only to set the bar higher at that time, until we obtain something else that we convince ourselves will make us happy. Using this "I'll Be Happy" strategy is only setting up our lives for failure to ever be completely happy, contented, or satisfied. If we cannot learn to be content with what we have now, then there will always be another "I'll Be Happy" goal around the corner, thereby rendering true happiness ultimately unattainable. Waiting to be happy is living in a constant state of suspension.

DID YOU EVER STOP TO ASK YOURSELF—

AM I HAPPY . . . OR CONTENT?

OR ARE YOUR DAYS SPENT ANTICIPATING

YOUR NEXT ACHIEVEMENT OR EVENT?

HAVE YOU POSTPONED TRUE SATISFACTION?

HAVE YOU REALLY BEEN AT PEACE?

OR HAVE YOU CREATED MEASUREMENTS FOR HAPPINESS

THAT NEVER SEEM TO CEASE?

A Round Tuit

On the top of any list of invisible fences, this word should appear: *procrastination*. It is the single most destructive impediment in the achievement of a goal or the realization of a dream.

One day when I was a child, my father had politely requested that I complete some mundane chore that apparently, I didn't find particularly interesting. I answered him curtly with my standard, "I'll do it, Dad . . . when I get around to it!" I couldn't help but notice the unmistakable smirk on his face as he reached into his pocket and handed me a little cardboard circle, about 2 inches in diameter. Both sides were printed with nothing but, *TUIT.*

He had, in essence, found a way of making sure I'd gotten a round tuit.

Procrastination is a cyclical flaw, because those who succumb to its immediate gratification are those who decide to stop procrastinating . . . tomorrow. Thus, the cycle continues. Realize that it is time to honestly identify the invisible fences and scale the hurdles that are stopping you from getting a round tuit.

Procrastination can be based on several things:

Disinterest: Once a project or goal is left untouched for a long period of time, the spark of enthusiasm wanes. Go back in time to tap into the source of initial inspiration and awaken the passion! Always keep inspiration handy. Magazine clippings, poems, quotes, articles . . . put them on a bulletin board, in your wallet, wherever you find most convenient. Place them in sight. It is amazing how powerfully inspirational the right words, at the right time, can be. Inspiration, wherever you find it, will help you to reclaim your vision.

Lethargy: If there is no underlying medical condition, the best cure for sluggishness is exercise! This issue is a recurring one . . . exercise increases your energy level, yet you feel as though you need an increased energy level to exercise. Many people view an exercise routine as having to be a time-consuming, breathless, arduous task. If scheduling an exercise routine is daunting and creates pressure, remove the word *routine* and just do it when you can. Fit it intermittently, but as often as possible, into your lifestyle. It can take just a few minutes a day to transform how you feel, mentally and physically. It is the easiest answer and the simplest method to use to achieve your goals and dreams.

Resolution Dissolution: This describes a steady decline in passion. You lose track of your focus because of the time that has passed between the initial spark of the idea and its commencement. You have put your goal on a back burner because it has aged, and new ideas entice you. Maybe you're thinking since you haven't acted upon it yet, it must not be as great as you'd believed it was initially. After all, there must be a reason you didn't act upon it yet, right? Not right. Your new idea will age just as fast. Do not replace old goals with newer ideas just because they have not been acted upon yet. If they are still on your mind, they will remain there until you begin working toward achieving them.

Duplicity: You tell yourself that tomorrow or next week you will start on your goal, project, or dream, but deep inside you know it's not the truth. In a way, we master the art of keeping secrets from ourselves. Are you lying to yourself to appease your mind and avoid disappointment or to keep a dream alive? By postponing your departure from the starting gate, you are postponing the race itself. Only by taking the first step can the race begin.

Support from Others (or Lack Thereof)

An effective way to immediately reduce your passion is to be around some-one who doesn't share the same fervent belief in an idea. I've read so many times that we need to eliminate the negative people from our lives. This is just not practical advice. What if the most negative person in your life is your own mother? You can't simply disown friends and family because they do not act as positively toward your ideas and objectives as you'd prefer. The truth is, if those around you don't believe in your goals and support your efforts to achieve them, you need to focus on minimizing their negative affects on your actions. Focus on your own confidence, perseverance, and belief in your ideals. If explaining how important they are to you and trying to involve the people around you as much as possible fails, reduce the time you spend with those who oppose. Don't waste large portions of your most precious commodity—your time—waiting for their approval and support. Remember, they have their own goals they are focusing their efforts toward achieving. Be willing to invest some attention in their projects and goals as well. Support is a reciprocal thing, and if you'd like people to invest in you, be willing to invest in them.

Perhaps friends and family are unwilling to lend assistance or support because you have been unwilling to openly consider their contributions in the past. Are you unyielding when their opinions and views differ from your own? If you ask for others' advice and ideas, be open and willing to consider them. If you follow a "my way or the highway" philosophy, then no one will want to work with or support you.

BE OPEN TO VIEWS AND SUGGESTIONS,

LET OTHERS FREELY SHED THEIR LIGHT;

TOO OFTEN THERE IS NOTHING LEFT,

WHEN YOU BELIEVE YOU'RE ALWAYS RIGHT.

COMPARISONS

As Oscar Wilde said, "Be yourself. Everyone else is taken."

We often compare ourselves to others, which can reinforce a negative self-image we've created. The people around us seem thinner, richer, happier. Society itself seems to have perfected its ability to brainwash us, too. We are inundated daily with TV commercials, print media, and radio ads suggesting how we "should" look, act, or live. That can make us feel like less than what we are because we are not living the idealistic lifestyle these images portray. There will always be someone "better" than you; and though you search for them less often, some people "worse" off than you. The end result of comparing yourself to others is that you wind up wishing you were different in some way. All of us are unique and born with different mindsets. We experience distinct interpretations of life and our reactions and emotions are vastly different. That's the way it is supposed to be. Our differences and our unique talents and abilities are what fuel the world. Your unique attributes represent important pieces to life's puzzle. Do not let the pride you feel be diminished by any contrast found in comparing yourself to another. Doing so likens you to a puppet by letting your actions and thoughts be controlled by another.

You have things that no one else can have or ever will have. Even identical twins have profoundly unique characteristics and qualities. No one is approaching perfection. Everyone has flaws and weaknesses, but the combination of the positive and the negative is what makes one person. Stop comparing what is you to what is them. You were meant to be a particular individual, YOU. Although this sounds as if it should be sung by a purple dinosaur on a kid's TV show—YOU are special! If you have forgotten who you are, then seek and find who you were meant to be in yourself, not in others. No one can be youer than you! Like grains of wood, we are each imperfect, unique, beautiful, and meant to go in our own directions.

Are you living your dash or living it for someone else? Our society suggests who we should become, how we should act, what we should buy, and even how we should dress. It is our responsibility to selectively ignore those suggestions. Once we make up our mind that we are here to live our own lives and not those of our parents, friends, teachers, and acquaintances, then we can live life based on our own talents, gifts, and passions.

When I approached the chapter of my life that involved having children, I envisioned them to be "mini me's." They would have my skills, my values, my ideals. They would walk like me, talk like me, and believe like me. It didn't take me very long to learn the error of my ways. Each of them, each of us, has been born with our own vastly unique abilities, cognitive skills, and unsown seeds. The key is to feel pride in all that is unique and special within us.

WHEN I THINK BACK ON THE CHILDHOOD QUESTION:

"WHEN YOU GROW UP, WHAT WILL YOU BE?"

IF I'D ONLY KNOWN THEN, WHAT I KNOW NOW,

I WOULD HAVE ANSWERED:

"I THINK I'LL BE ME . . ."

GRAY AREA

Learn to differentiate fantasies (hopes, desires, wishes) from goals (objectives, ambitions, purpose) and dreams (thoughts, visions, ideas). Identify your ambitions and aspirations and weigh the potential investment of effort it would take to achieve them against statistical odds. Evaluate their attainability, and then eliminate the fantasies. Winning the lottery would, of course, be a wonderful objective to meet, but would it not be a more productive use of your time to evaluate the odds, face the truth, and label this one and similar imaginary scenarios a fantasy instead of a dream or a goal? Fantasies are fun, but when they actually require an investment of real time, they represent an invisible fence and impede the journey toward a goal.

To assist in identifying and evaluating goals, dreams, and fantasies, remember that a realization of a goal or dream is more likely to represent a sincere investment of time and effort rather than luck, happenstance, or fate. When you mix high aspirations with reality and feasibility, rather than hope and fantasy, the result is an attainable goal.

I've heard many people share the sayings "Nothing is impossible" and "Become a possibilitarian." While the meaning is well intentioned, and it is most definitely positive to remain open to all possibilities, we have to understand that everything is, in fact, not possible. In reality, the phrases above are simply based on blind faith and denial. Suppose I had two objectives in mind, the first being to lose fifty pounds and the second to become president of the United States. Both technically are "possible," but if I deal in real, I soon realize that only one is truly attainable for me with hard work and dedication. I could spend 100 percent of the rest of my life striving to be elected, but feasibly speaking, it probably wouldn't happen. Yet, I could put down a cheeseburger or two and reach the first of the two scenarios. Realistically, there are more things that cannot happen than can. Therefore, we need to focus completely on what *can* happen, be ourselves, and appreciate our accomplishments and capabilities.

When you differentiate your goals from your dreams, you are able to set realistic goals. When our goals are founded upon fantasies, rather than attainable objectives, we set ourselves up for frustration. Most of us can achieve more than we initially think possible—aim just beyond what feels realistic and be sure you are striving to attain goals because they will make you feel more accomplished, successful, satisfied, or whole, not because you are trying to impress others.

DITHERING

Many people confuse dithering with procrastinating. Though the two invisible fences may intersect, they are separate obstacles. To dither is to vacillate, to be hesitant and indecisive. Though dithering leads to procrastinating because the more time you waste trying to decide something, the more time is spent doing nothing productive, you can't achieve your goals until you identify what they are. Blindly moving forward in the direction of your dreams, hoping the objectives will present themselves as the journey unfolds, is a positive action, but an ineffective one at best. If you are an indecisive person, sketch your plan in pencil and have an eraser handy.

Start by writing down aspects of your goal. You don't have to begin with a perfect, chronological plan. Get the floating thoughts out of your mind and onto the paper. When I started writing this book, my thoughts and ideas were like a box of open spaghetti that had been dropped from thirty feet. They were scattered everywhere. Whenever I began to write stories, they would meander around my mind, disrupt my focus, and stop the continuous creative flow. Not until I emptied them onto paper in briefly titled ideas did I make room so that the creative process could begin.

The Jinx

There are those who believe that if they honestly surrender to feelings of happiness and sincere heartfelt gratitude for the blessings in their lives, they will somehow "jinx" their run of good fortune. They believe that if they fully succumb to realizing and absorbing all they have to be thankful for, it will cause someone or something to push a needle through their balloon of contentment.

For some, the jinx scenario is founded on a belief system of measured entitlement—when people believe that they are allotted fixed quantities of happiness, and that there is a minimum and maximum of happiness that they can achieve. Perhaps this idea is founded on guilt from lack of unselfish giving or subconscious opposition to the idea of karma.

Those whose hearts are filled with the by-products of magnanimity—personal pride and self-satisfaction—are wishfully anticipating, but not expecting, reciprocity from the universe for their kind deeds. Those who believe the world does not give back more freely to those who give selflessly are generally in need of oil to lubricate the rusty door hinges on their hearts from being opened so infrequently. If you don't give, begin to give. If you do give, give more. I'm not referring to your money but to your time, your love, and your compassion. Do good things and good deeds, and you will be paying the imaginary dues that may be preventing you from enjoying your lifetime subscription to joy.

If the invisible fence, this idea of a jinx, describes you even a little, then it is an invisible fence that needs to be torn down. If the fear that what you reap is based upon what you sow and you've yet to hoe a row, then implement change immediately. Then you will begin to eliminate any guilt and doubt that you are entitled to as many blessings and as much happiness as can fill a life.

Many believe, as I do, that if you do good things—for whatever reasons—you can confidently select a seat on the roundtrip karma train because good deeds will come back to you eventually. (As long as your anticipation of this fact is not the motive behind the initial kind deed.)

DELEGATION

Seek assistance; ask for help if you need it. Don't assume people will see you drowning. Yell for a life preserver before you go down. People cannot read your mind. I'm reminded of the joke, "All those who believe in Telekinesis, raise my hand."

Of the immeasurable words of wisdom my father bequeathed upon me, one particular cliché undoubtedly did me more harm than good. As a workaholic, he would always say, "If you want something done right, do it yourself." The word *delegate* never entered his vocabulary. The result was that I would (and still have a tendency to) try to do it all myself. I found it easier to accept and rectify errors I'd made myself, rather than receiving flak for errors that were not my own but for which I was still held ultimately responsible. Unfortunately I left the corporate world before I learned the magic—and the necessity of—delegating. Admitting you're overwhelmed and need assistance is not a weakness.

What keeps you from delegating or requesting assistance? Is it the fear of accepting responsibility and blame if failure is the result of "sharing" a responsibility, or is it an unwillingness to share the praise if the outcome is a success? Too often people abuse the intended purpose of delegation and view it instead as an immediate transference of responsibility and, thus, accountability. They use a "pass the buck" strategy to avoid personal responsibility and dodge repercussions for their actions.

I'VE FOUND THAT IT IS ALWAYS BEST

TO ACCEPT RESPONSIBILITY . . .

TO "FESS UP WHEN YOU MESS UP"

IS THE BEST PHILOSOPHY!

Have you ever watched a flock of birds flying in one direction? Through teamwork, they are able to turn suddenly in unison and fly as one unit in an entirely new direction without a hiccup in formation. Learning to work together with others to accomplish a goal, even though you may feel you have more to contribute than they do, is a sure road to success. If you make an exception to the old adage "There is no 'I' in team," by stating that there is, however, a "me" if you rearrange the letters a little, then you need to ask yourself why you feel the need to be recognized more than the others who have contributed? Is this the reason behind your hesitation to delegate? If you wonder why you should invest time and hard work if you're not the one being recognized, consider the importance of personal pride and satisfaction discovered in an accomplished goal, even if it required support from others to achieve. An athlete, though often selected for accolades, does not score points without the help of his team. There is an old saying: "If you're walking along a fence and spot a turtle sitting atop a fencepost, you know he didn't get there by himself!"

VARIABLES

I can remember desperately pleading my case to Mrs. Thompson in elementary school after my dog did, in fact, eat my homework. Hey, it happens! She was an unusually kindhearted woman, and thus, the distrust she expressed in my earnest statement was curious to me. I didn't understand why she refused to understand. What about VARIABLES, people? Plans and goals are wonderful to strive toward and even better to achieve, but there are variables that are out of our control that actually occur, and they can prevent us from getting the job done.

Every company I've ever worked for would perform annual reviews on their employees, rating performance and insisting that we should set our goals for the following year, in writing, in three days. These goals would be used as the personal and professional achievements against which our performance would be measured at our next annual review. After I became a working mother, I soon realized that many of what I would list as goals may not be achievable because of my own little variables. Their needs, lives, and requirements would no doubt involve many adjustments to my goals, which is a fact I completely understood and accepted without hesitation when I agreed to enter the hood (motherhood). Each year, I would begin, without fail, to describe my first goal: *To create a comprehensive list of goals for my annual review.* My bosses never found the humor in my attempt at levity.

Those in positions of authority, including many parents, often refuse to believe there could, at times, be a reasonable explanation for an unachieved task or goal. Somehow, they feel that it diminishes their level of power in some way to acknowledge that there are variables beyond our control. Even in a court of law, people are initially presumed innocent.

However, we need to stop relying on variables as excuses. In order to learn how to not repeat past failures and move forward, we have to forget the variables. We have to learn to swallow them, along with a piece of our pride, each time we fail.

Stop practicing the blame game. In order to be a successful, content, progressive person, practice bringing events in your life back to you. Whenever your instinct is to cast responsibility elsewhere, remember that your decisions are made by you, not another person. Though someone's actions in the past may have influenced your beliefs and emotions to date, choices and decisions are made solely by you. Stop blaming others when the results or repercussions from your choices, actions, and decisions are less than expected or anticipated. How long will you let what *was* continue to affect what *is*?

COASTING

Coasting is going along, never making waves, never attempting change. Time passes and we become complacent and content to coast our lives through a perpetual no-wake zone. When we allow ourselves to coast, we drift further and further away from our objectives. We don't even realize how far we've drifted until we see the distance between where we are now and where we want to be. When we coast, we become complacent, and what was once stimulating becomes tedious. We know enjoyment is here, but we just don't feel it. We become conditioned to our current situation and surroundings.

It can be helpful to create a personal contract with yourself. When you sign a contract to make payments or provide a service, the act of signing your name to a promise—a commitment—allows you the power to prioritize the task. It has been proven to be an effective tool in inspiring others involved in your project, as well. Just as you sign a contract to promise others a specific goal, make that promise to yourself. A self-contract can create a cattle-prod type of relationship that can provide continued encouragement and accountability.

SIDE TRAILS

If you're the type who likes to begin a trip knowing only the destination and not the twists and turns involved in the journey, at least decide on mile markers, where you can stop, evaluate, and reroute your path if necessary on the way toward your goal. Mile markers can enable you to avoid the detours, distractions, and side trails that present themselves at every turn.

To ensure that you avoid these side trails, do something in the mindset toward achieving your goal every day. Do *something*. A writing instructor once told me to hang a big "year-at-a-glance" calendar prominently on my office wall. He said to buy a big, thick, red magic marker and for each day that I completed my task of writing, I should place a big red *X* across the square representing that day. In just a few days, I had created a recognizable chain, and the more I wrote, the longer it grew. My task then was not to break the chain.

Tenacity and focus are important allies in the battle against invisible fences. To remain focused requires tenacity, and becoming tenacious requires focus. Another suggestion I was given with regard to writing, my chosen vocation, was in reference to the slow fade of enthusiasm that seemed to take place in the midst of my efforts to complete a lengthy project. I would begin the same project several different times and fail to complete it for various reasons. The more unsuccessful attempts I experienced, the more discouraged I would become. A professor in a writing class suggested that I apply imaginary chair glue to the chair where I would sit to write. She suggested that I pretend my bottom was stuck to the chair with this chair glue until the project was complete.

Naturally, if attaining your goal doesn't require sitting for hours at a time, find the comparison of chair glue to use. Imagine similar tools that would mentally encourage you to attain the stick-to-itiveness necessary to accomplish your ambitions and objectives. Find quiet time whenever necessary, eliminate outside influences, and reach inside to remember the time when you believed in yourself and your project.

A story that continues to inspire me is that of the wolf. I've read that a majority of the wolves' hunting expeditions end in failure to produce prey. Hence the creation of the phrase "hungry like the wolf." Yet, each attempt, each unsuccessful endeavor, hones the wolf's hunting skills and fuels his desire. He learns from each error and perfects his skills. He is not deterred, not discouraged, but uses what he has learned to continue to hunt—stronger, faster, and wiser.

"Some succeed because they are destined to.
Others succeed because they are determined to."
—Henry Van Dyke

One simple stanza I wrote inspires me repeatedly when I become lukewarm about a particular aspiration.

WHEN YOU THINK YOU'VE GIVEN ALL YOU CAN GIVE,

STRIVE TO GIVE JUST A LITTLE BIT MORE . . .

OFTEN THE VERY LAST KEY THAT HANGS ON A RING

IS THE ONE THAT WILL OPEN THE DOOR!

HIDDEN INSPIRATION

Keep what inspires you within your sight. Photographs, books, quotes . . . whatever fuels the fires of your imagination and encourages you to move forward, place it where it will be seen regularly. The moment you put it on a high shelf or in a drawer, you block the view to that which will inspire you to reach your aspirations.

When I was entering seventh grade, the schedule of classes included an option for guitar lessons. I eagerly signed up and counted the days until school began so that I could learn to play, something I'd always yearned to do. I received a call the day before school started and was informed the class was no longer being offered due to non-participation. I can still feel the disappointment. Years passed, and I never took lessons, never bought a guitar, never revisited the aspiration. This year, my daughter surprised me with the gift of a guitar. After hours of practicing rudimentary lessons, I serenaded everyone on Christmas morning with repeated rousing renditions of "Jingle Bells!" Though I knew I was in the beginning stages of playing, I felt pride, and I felt excited because a vision I'd buried had been resurrected. Now I have revived my goal of learning to play, in spite of its being hidden for years. The guitar's presence itself will inspire me daily as I pass by it every day on my way from room to room.

The old saying "out of sight, out of mind" is so very accurate when it comes to staying inspired and keeping your train of thought securely on track.

Close Enough

I have always been a person who continually strives for perfection. I remember as a child, slowly and methodically outlining a drawing with a thick black crayon so the different colors wouldn't "bleed" outside the lines. Because, if by chance, one color spilled onto another while under the control of my small hand, though my picture may have been nearing completion, I would crumple it up and throw it away. In my mind, it was no longer of use because it was no longer perfect, and to me, it only represented personal failure.

Looking back, I don't know where the root of that pressure came from as my parents never placed unduly high expectations upon me nor were they perfection-seekers in their own lives. It was not a trait I'd inherited, but one I'd adopted and perfected in a few short years, and it has taken more time than that to "unlearn" it.

As I've grown older, I've recognized the unnecessary pressure most of us experience in the day-to-day struggles of life. The word *pressure* is defined as "powerful and stressful demands on somebody's time, attention, and energy." In my view, there are two types of pressure: the kind that life places on us through no choice of our own and that which we willingly place upon ourselves.

In this world of wannabe overachievers, I realize my "Close Enough" idea will perhaps be perceived by some as having been inspired by a lack of ambition. However, I feel that it is derived more from a theory of building self-confidence and finding the positives in every failure.

In business, and society in general, we are consistently advised that in order to achieve "success," we must set high personal and professional goals. After doing so, we are then expected to spend much of our precious time devising strategies to assist us in achieving these self-made objectives in order that we may avoid, like the plague, personal failure. Alas, failure leads to guilt. Guilt leads to remorse. Remorse leads to regret. It is a cycle of doom that we ourselves create!

Although we set high goals with great intentions, the backfire effect is that we are often left with feelings of failure when those initial goals are not able to be met, often due to circumstances beyond our control. In my view, the bar is often set too high initially based on a subconscious calculation made up of 40% zeal, 30% expectation, 25% optimism, with just 5% left to fate.

I've established many goals for myself, but for each I've learned to create an imaginary ladder of success. On this ladder, I've installed an extra rung just before reaching the pinnacle of each—my Close Enough rung. If my best efforts bring me to that point and not beyond, I've learned to not diminish my efforts by being dissatisfied with the result, thereby allowing myself to be content with my accomplishment. This allows me to not merely anticipate the arrival at each destination, but to enjoy the ride.

I'm not at all saying that we should settle for mediocrity or "good enough." I'm saying Go for the Gold, always, but if Silver is your fortune, accept it, be proud of it, learn from it, and let it go. There is a difference between reaching Close Enough and settling for good enough.

Confucious said, "When it is obvious that the goals cannot be reached, don't adjust the goals, adjust the action steps." I agree with the intention of this quote, but I disagree with the undue pressure such an ideal places in our mindset. We should not consider ourselves as having failed if we find it necessary to adjust our goals in light of developing changes and unanticipated variables. I suggest establishing BE FLEXIBLE as the first goal to reach, so that you may work from there. Value and significance can be found in an unmet goal. Shortcomings offer infinite opportunities from which to learn and invaluable lessons to take with us. A lesson taught verbally cannot begin to equal one that is learned from experiences, mistakes, and blunders. A mistake is the most efficient method to unveil a weakness and turn it into a strength.

Some might say being proud of achieving an altered goal would represent false pride. Again, I must disagree. That thought process only reinforces my belief that we place undue stress and pressure upon ourselves. We need to learn to establish attainable, yet challenging, goals that will not leave us with feelings of disappointment, thereby diminishing the confidence we have in our abilities.

My daughter argued the point by stating that lowering your standards in order to achieve a goal nulls your objective and defeats the purpose. But if you set unrealistic goals or are inflexible to modify previously set goals to better match current circumstance, then failure is your fate, regardless. I've learned not to strive for as a goal but to be satisfied with reaching the Close Enough rung. If opportunities arise for you to continue beyond, on your way to reaching the pinnacle, do so with vehemence. But if this rung is ultimately, after exhaustive efforts, your accomplishment, step upon it with pride and consider it a triumph. Yes, my Close Enough theory could be construed as the equivalent of accepting a "B," when striving for an "A," but if you can mentally translate that "B" to stand for the "Best" you could do given your current circumstances, what more is there? Why further punish yourself? Grant yourself: PERmission to be imPERfect.

Learn to be less hard on yourself so that you may enjoy the essence of life instead of constantly focusing most of your time and energy on your next achievement. Why not set goals that are challenging and attainable so that you may, more often, feel the pride of achievement? Those driven by their own definitions of success would undoubtedly argue that it's imperative to set high goals in order to become "successful." I realize it's important to challenge ourselves, sometimes beyond our own limitations. However, I also think we should weigh the investment of time, energy, and that which we forfeit from our journey during the pursuit, against the accomplishment of each goal, to ensure it is fully worth the sacrifice.

I'VE LEARNED TO ENSURE, AS I STRUGGLE

TO REACH EVERY ESTABLISHED GOAL,

THAT EACH BRIDGE OF SUCCESS

I'M ATTEMPTING TO CROSS

IS FULLY WORTH PAYING ITS TOLL!

I once worked for a high-ranking naval-reserve officer. On his wall was a framed quote that read: "No one cares about the storms you encountered at sea, only that you brought the ship to port." Another boss I had further into my career often stated a similar idea in a joking manner: "Spare me the labor pains, show me the baby!" I've always wrestled with the concept these light-hearted statements represent. Life is ever changing, and circumstances arise that prevent us from achieving goals and objectives, no matter how much effort we put forth. Abiding by these statements would mean that an investment of 100 percent effort would be in vain and would not matter if the ultimate goal were not met with 100 percent success. I feel that recognition is a necessity, even if you are the only person to recognize yourself. I refuse to believe there is no value in spent sweat and struggle. Remember the effort, realize there is courage and value in the attempt, and don't let failure discourage you. Use the information you've learned to move forward, stronger and better than before.

In summary, do set goals. Set them high. However, do not beat yourself up if your efforts bring you only to the Close Enough rung on the ladder. Realize that Close Enough, while perhaps not preferred, is not unacceptable. In the game of horseshoes, Close Enough often wins.

DO NOT BELITTLE AN EARNEST ENDEAVOR

THOUGH YOU MAY NOT HAVE PREVAILED . . .

IF YOU HAVE LEARNED FROM YOUR ERRORS,

MY FRIEND, YOU HAVE NOT FAILED!

ON
GRATITUDE

Stratitude

Strategy: a plan of action or policy designed to achieve an overall purpose or intention. **Gratitude:** the quality of being thankful; readiness to show appreciation. **Stratitude:** an imaginary technique whereby one learns to combine these two in order to adopt, hone, and maintain a personal strategy of gratitude.

I consider true gratitude a skill or an art—a trait that is not inherent but acquired during the course of life's journey. Furthermore, I've come to understand that it is the very core of achieving tranquility, contentment, and peace in life. Without it, there is an indiscernible unrest . . . a nagging, consistent inner turmoil. I compare it to constant ripples in the waters of our soul in lieu of smooth, still springs.

I am referring to those haunting, taunting ripples caused by desire. Desire is gratitude's nemesis—a silent enemy that hounds us unrelentingly, teasing us with the "what could be," while simultaneously squelching our appreciation for the "what is." Not until we learn to retire desire and include gratitude can we calm these ripples of unrest.

To do this, we must first adopt a technique I've titled "Stratitude." This is obviously the result of combining the two words: *strategy* and *gratitude*.

Stratitude is a focus . . . an attention given to "what is." It is a concentration: a deliberate devotion to absolute appreciation. It is an acceptance: a recognition and absorption of one's personal reality. It is a slow-down: a deceleration of our high-speed lives allowing us to drink in the often-transient blessings that are present in our "now." It is a reversal of a thought process: a philosophy created by society's altered views of success, which may have become ingrained in our minds. It is a willingness: a readiness to open our hearts and minds to truly seize what is available in our "here." It is a realization: an awareness that failures and disappointments are not only blessings in disguise, but also important, necessary life lessons. It is a belief: a heartfelt certainty that the phrase "enough is enough" is not a cliché, but an earnest truth.

Stratitude, once achieved, can literally make what is old and familiar new and worthwhile again. It can bring alive our spirits through a satisfaction that is all-too-often repressed by wants and wishes.

I'm not saying it's healthier not to try to attain higher levels of success. I'm saying we need to learn to be content during our time spent on THIS level, while striving to advance to the next. We need to find our own healthy balance of appreciation and desire. Because it is when desire overcomes appreciation that we experience that inconsistency of thought the ever-present splinter of dissatisfaction, which can pierce the outer skin of our life's reality, morphing our "what is" into an unfeasible "what could be," a sometimes unattainable "what should be," or an often rueful "what would be." When more desire than appreciation is present, invisible chains wrap around our psyche that prevent us from moving freely forward while ensuring that the threshold of real happiness remains just beyond our reach.

It is easier to attain a high level of Stratitude if you can practice consciously reducing your use of the word *if* in regular conversation. If is often accompanied by negativity, which reverses the positive effects of Stratitude. If only I would have = what could be. If only this would have happened = what should be. If this had not happened = what would be. The ifs make it a more difficult struggle to fully accept the "what is." If you can truly master and adopt a strategy of gratitude, i.e., stratitude, it can change your life forever. It is our self-created personal dissatisfaction with ourselves, our positions, and our relationships that fuels our inner turmoil and unrest.

Gratitude and appreciation are in reaching peace of mind. They form the very foundation upon which you can build lasting contentment for your soul, for your self, for your life—a unique contentment only experienced when you can honestly feel thankfulness and satisfaction within yourself, simultaneously. It is a contentment that warrants the repeated use of the phrase "Thank You." It is good practice to repeat that phrase each and every day, because there is always something present in our lives for which we can be thankful. Just who should you thank for the blessings that are present in your life? Thank God, thank yourself, thank your parents, thank the universe, thank goodness, thank your lucky stars . . . thank whomever or whatever you choose as the object of your gratitude, but show it, realize it, feel it.

Time is one of our greatest current blessings . . . so why not try using more of it, being thankful for what is, as well as less of it regretting what was or yearning for what isn't. Expressing gratitude for our blessings on a regular basis is a proven method for increasing feelings of inner peace.

"I don't really care whether my glass is half full or half empty . . .
I'm just happy to have a glass."
—Joe Farrel

PICTURE IT GONE

For every aspect of your life where you find dissatisfaction, pretend—just for a moment—it isn't there. Imagine the source of this feeling gone from your days completely. If you're finding your teenager disagreeable, imagine life without him or her. If you and your spouse are not in harmony, think of waking up tomorrow without him or her in your life. If your house is in need of repair or renovation and causing you anxiety, picture yourself standing in a cold rain with no front door to walk through. If your job is a cause of stress and angst, imagine being among the thousands of unemployed.

Imagining something is gone forever forces you to appreciate what is here. Have you ever awoken from a realistic, heart-wrenching nightmare or a powerfully true-to-life bad dream? Those few minutes when you become consciously aware of the truth, that what you've experienced so real in your mind is not indeed a reality can be described as nothing more than absolute appreciation. If we could only remember and relive the "afterdream" feelings of thankfulness that fill those fleeting moments, it would help us to achieve our stratitude.

Live Your Dash.

THOSE

I write, not for those thankful
for an abundance of wealth,
for whom good fortune has blessed
their home and their health;

those who walk golden pathways
toward means and success . . .
a safe distance apart
from those who have less,

but instead for the people
who can see those with more
and still humbly count blessings
for which they are thankful for;

those whose journey through life
has been far from the best,
yet consider themselves
nonetheless, blessed;

those whose open hearts give
without asking why;
those who freely share water
when their own well is dry;

those who view neighbors' riches
with no envy or greed,
nor resent them for having
much more than they need.

Let us solemnly promise
a day shall not close
without being grateful
and thankful for Those . . .

Every Single Day

My poem, "Every Single Day," was inspired by one of my father's favorite sayings. In a joking manner, he would often say that it would be better if each of us were each born with an expiration date stamped on our forehead, like a carton of milk. In that way, we could better plan the route we chose to take during our journey on Earth, as we would know definitively the date of our ultimate departure.

My father taught me invaluable lessons about truly living my life while he was in the midst of losing his own. He taught me that we are not guaranteed a tomorrow and that many of us will not have the opportunity that he was given to know our approximate "expiration date." We need to tell our loved ones how we feel as often as we can and not wait until tomorrow. These days are so hectic and busy, and minutes dissipate into hours and days before our very eyes. That is why we need to learn to slow down enough to fully experience this life and appreciate the blessings with which we are granted. Then, and only then, will we be able to truly live . . . Every Single Day.

EVERY SINGLE DAY

Though we may battle our opponent, time,
someday we must admit defeat.
As the days run into weeks . . . and years,
too soon, a lifetime is complete.

But if the span of every lifetime
were cut into pieces with a knife,
then every single day would be
. . . a single slice of life.

And we'd be certain of the days we have
to laugh, to love . . . to live,
knowing just how much to take from life
. . . and just how much to give.

We'd divide our time accordingly,
say and do the things we'd need
because every single day to us
would then be, guaranteed.

But life is not indefinite;
time continues its forward stride . . .
and it may end before the laughter's done
and all the tears are cried.

So do what you feel you have to do
and say what you need to say.
Seize all the life contained within
every single day.

Say "I Love You" more often,
than just every now and then . . .
for you may not have the chance tomorrow
to say it once again.

Don't put off true happiness.
Don't put your hopes and dreams on a shelf.
Live every single day
as if it were a lifetime in itself.

ORDINARY DAYS

I once had a conversation with my friend, whose mom has been bravely battling cancer. Her mom had mentioned to her that when my friend was growing up, they had a special set of dishes that was set aside to be used only on very special occasions. My friend vaguely remembered images in her mind of those "special" dishes. As a child, she could only catch a glimpse of their decorative rims as even on tiptoes, her little neck could stretch barely high enough to view their neatly stacked piles on a top shelf in the cabinet. She also recalled that the contents of that shelf were to be considered untouchable. However, her mom told her that since she has been facing this challenge in her life, those same dishes are now proudly displayed upon her dinner table on a regular basis, and she deeply regrets not enjoying their beauty on even the most ordinary days of the past.

I began thinking about the phrase "ordinary days." I couldn't escape the thought that so many of us bundle and individually count down the days until our next notable happening or event, that we dismiss those days in between and tend to label them as "ordinary." Often we will discount them as though they have less value than those times when something exciting is scheduled to happen in our life.

I've been guilty of this so many times myself, saying, "Only fourteen days left until . . . " In hindsight, it seemed as though if I had nothing special scheduled or anticipated—no vacation, no holiday, not even a package in the mail—I had a tendency to consider the day "ordinary." I found that I would often endure this type of day as if it were some sort of task instead of living it to the fullest, considering it nothing more than a stepping stone leading to a bigger, better day.

I've begun a whole new way of thinking in my life and that is that no day should be considered ordinary. Every morning that the sun rises and we wake up should be considered special. If you view every single day with this mindset and adopt the attitude that each day is literally a single slice of life—not just twenty-four hours to live to bring you closer to some special happening or event—then you can learn to appreciate and experience all that is contained within each and every day.

I've often pondered the notion at the end of a day on which I've slept far too late or sat lifelessly staring at the television for hours that I will undoubtedly yearn to have these misspent hours back in the years to come. Never a truer statement has been made than "youth is wasted on the young." I encourage you to spend more of your precious hours focusing on the "extra" in every extraordinary day.

Ordinary: a commonplace condition or situation.

Is there anything common about the way the sun slowly appears over the horizon? Is there anything common about the bright and blending hues of the leaves as they change in the fall? Is there anything common about the way the rays of a sunburst form a perfect pattern as they gently force their way through the clouds and illuminate the surrounding sky as if designed by some computer-graphics program? All of these extraordinary events, and so many more, happen on ordinary days. When we learn to realize the uniqueness and beauty found in each day, then we can truly understand that no day is ever ordinary.

THANK GOD, IT'S . . . TUESDAY?

T.G.I.T.!! Doesn't quite have the same ring to it, now does it? I doubt you will hear the question, "Is it Tuesday yet?" repeated much around the office, either. THAT, my friends, is precisely why I have decided to write a story in defense of Tuesday! (That, and the fact that it apparently lacks the conviction to stand up for itself.) I truly believe Tuesday has not been fully appreciated in the lives of many . . . most, I'd venture to say.

Tuesdays have simply been overlooked. However, considering that Tuesday literally represents 1/7th of our lives, or slightly more than 14 percent (I did the math myself after googling how to convert a fraction into a percentage), I've begun to change my thinking and have been, as of late, anticipating and celebrating my Tuesdays! Tuesdays have just gotten a bum rap. Whether negative or positive, all of the other days during the week have a role, a position, a niche in life. In my mind, Tuesday conjures up images of that skinny guy on the beach who always got sand kicked in his face by the bodybuilder. (If that commercial was before your time, my sincere apologies.)

Monday: The first day of the workweek. It may not be the most anticipated or enjoyable day of the week, but at least it has that going for it! Many times Monday is included as part of a three-day holiday weekend, thereby, forcing Tuesday to step up as a pinch hitter and take the wrath as the dreaded "funsucker" day that comes after the long weekend.

Tuesday: Uhm . . . well. (I couldn't even find accolades to merit a bold font.)

Wednesday: This day holds the deed on some prime real estate, lying smack-dab in the middle of the workweek. The day even has its own nickname, "Humpday," used in the context of climbing a proverbial hill to get through a rough week. (*Tuesday* doesn't have a nickname.)

Thursday: Though it isn't the end of the workweek, people look forward to Thursday due to its proximity to Friday. Thursday has it made. Many times when Friday is included in a three-day weekend, Thursday becomes the pinch hitter for Friday, and, therefore, receives all the awe and admiration usually bestowed upon that day.

Friday: This lucky day holds esteem and power. It is equivalent to the CEO of the workweek. (I believe if Friday were to take on a life-form, it would have tremendous confidence and an inflated ego.) There are few who don't relish Friday, being the last of the five days that makes one "weak." Even the famous nursery rhyme, chimes: "Friday's child is loving and giving . . ." (Probably because it is typically a payday.)

Saturday: Need I say more? Just repeating the word makes your mouth curl into a subconscious smile. Saturday—I even smiled as I typed the *S*, anticipating the letters that were to follow—is quite possibly the most popular day of the week. That is because the word *Saturday* has become synonymous with the word *fun*. Fun happens on Saturday. Weddings, parties, and picnics are planned for Saturday. In fact, I'm surprised they didn't just go ahead and name it Funday. (This may have been a deliberate oversight to avoid confusion, as it would have then rhymed with its successors: Funday, Sunday, Monday.)

Sunday: Day of worship for many and rest for most. Sunday has a reputation as a respected, revered, and well-regarded day. Fine lunches are often planned for Sunday. If days were coins, Sunday would be the most valuable. It is, after all, the only one of the seven days whose first syllable commands such respect on the celestial sphere that others must orbit around it.

So, aside from being a day on which we cast votes for politicians we may later regret, what does Tuesday own that is special and unique? A travel site states that, according to their Web site statistics, Tuesday seems to be the most popular day amongst office-goers for daydreaming about their next holiday or vacation. That, in itself, says a lot about Tuesday.

Of course, there is always the voters' Super Tuesday, history's Black Tuesday, and Mardi Gras' Fat Tuesday . . . but what about just plain ole Tuesday? It doesn't have a reputation of its own based purely on the generic day itself. It wouldn't even qualify for a decent parking space in a workweek parking lot—it would probably be the space in the back . . . under the trees . . . where the birds congregate.

Assuming an average life span of an estimated seventy to eighty years, that grants us approximately 3,900 Tuesdays. Following this pattern, I have spent around 2,444 Tuesdays with about 1,456 remaining, if I'm so blessed. (I'm wondering how many of my readers are trying to calculate my age at this point. . . .)

From now on, we should look forward to each and every Tuesday. Make special plans on Tuesday. I plan to make the next 1,456 Tuesdays so memorable that they will make up for the 2,444 Tuesdays I've simply overlooked or counted the hours until they could be marked from my calendar. In fact, if I were granted a wish, I'd ask to have all those Tuesdays added back to my life's account . . . and take the opportunity to live them once again.

Why not vow today to never take another Tuesday for granted?

AOKs

Acts of Kindness: selfless acts performed to either assist or add joy to another individual's day, life, or attitude. They are the smaller gestures of benevolence, thoughtfulness, and consideration that are spoken or given to or for the benefit of another. Whether planned in advance or spontaneous, I call them "AOKs," and I simply delight in performing them when opportunities present themselves to me. A true AOK is performed without any expectation or realization of reciprocation, recognition, acknowledgement, or gratitude.

There are so many chances to offer these kind gestures while just going about our daily business. My mind has subconsciously become a watchtower, always on the lookout for AOK opportunities. Contributions to society through various avenues of charity in large quantities are admirable, but the immeasurable value of small Acts of Kindness should never be discounted, because they have the ability to create big differences in little ways.

Carrying out an act of kindness produces unique and wonderful feelings. Harold Kushner wrote, "It is as though something inside your body responds and says, yes, this is how I ought to feel." Bestowing a gentle smile, a kind word, earnest praise, or lending a listening ear is like planting a seed and having the added benefit of watching it instantly blossom. Though kind words are softly spoken—short and sweet—their echo can remain in the receiver's mind forever.

Grandiose, well-publicized offerings are honorable and noteworthy, but true kindness is silent, often secret, and doesn't expect recognition. If you require an audience as incentive to perform an AOK, then it is truly not an act of altruism, but egotism. The most gratifying AOKs are the ones performed when no one is looking—those that are not weighed on a scale of self-interest, those that are performed, proceeded by a satisfied smile while walking away.

However, there is no shame in feeling personal pride from an AOK. It doesn't turn an unselfish act selfish if you feel good about doing it. Allow yourself some pride and satisfaction when you help others. As long as the motive for performing an act of kindness is pure, what does it matter if you silently find delight in what you've accomplished? If performing a true AOK compels you to give yourself an "attaboy!" pat on the back or just some silent applause, then so be it. There is no harm in recognizing yourself for a kind deed. The harm is when you expect the recognition to come from others. If all you are doing is trying to accumulate more points on the karma scoreboard, it diminishes the thoughtful intent and belittles the action itself.

AOKs involve opening the heart. So often, the heart can close its doors in response to sadness, loss, pain, or fear. Kindness is the key that will open it again. Inner peace will expand and thrive when a heart becomes receptive and giving once again.

> *"Kindness is a language which the deaf*
> *can hear and the blind can see."*
> —Mark Twain

RIPPLES

Much like the expanding ripples that appear when you throw a stone into a pond of still water, the effect of a kind deed travels and extends well beyond the point of origin, growing progressively larger. Your single good deed, big or small, has the potential to inspire others and cause a chain of kindness that will continue to lengthen itself as others are linked through their own acts of benevolence. Whether we each perform them with the intent to benefit others; for our own conscience, heart, and soul; to affirm our feelings of self-worth; because they feel right; or because they are right, performing Acts of Kindness perpetuates thoughtfulness and compassion. AOKs create a heightened level of awareness by opening our hearts wider in order to give more. It stands to reason a heart that is opened wider to give, will have more room as well, to receive.

One of my most gratifying aspects of performing acts of kindness thus far was watching an incident involving my youngest daughter. I realized with pride, through emotional osmosis, my love of AOKs had permeated her lifestyle. We were at a grocery store we visit frequently when an elderly woman standing in line in front of us dropped her change purse. Coins scattered everywhere across the floor of the store, reaching all the way under the candy shelves. The woman, in obvious distress, stated, "Oh, I'm so clumsy!" But within seconds, my nine-year-old had dropped to her knees to begin gathering every coin she could find to return to the woman. Without a word, she unassumingly handed the money to the woman, who was obviously touched and impressed by my child's immediate reaction. So often, it's these little gestures that bring a smile and brighten someone's day.

Whether they are acts of generosity, heroism, unselfishness, or charity, performing AOKs will lift you up, make you smile, and offer the opportunity to reflect upon them later, bringing forth moments of personal satisfaction.

"Beginning today, treat everyone you meet as if they were going to be dead by midnight. Extend to them all the care, kindness, and understanding you can muster, and do it with no thought of any reward. Your life will never be the same again."

—Og Mandino

Live Your Dash.

FAMILY IN NEED

"Family in Need" read the handwritten note.
"Give in the Name of the Lord."
It was posted in the main hallway
in the center of the bulletin board.

As parishioners passed through the hall
after the Sunday worshipping session,
they stopped to read the prominent note
and formed a concerned expression.

Many met out in the parking lot
in groups of two and three
as they spoke of this family in need
and wondered just who it could be.

Did this family attend their church?
What was their situation?
Just which family had the preacher met
who was in need of such donation?

They spoke a while and left for home,
but not until they all agreed
that they would gather everything they could
for this family in need.

The preacher was sitting in the office
ready to accept the gifts bestowed,
and he stood up straight to warmly greet
the first family that showed.

The little boy stepped up to the table
with a football in his hands.
He said, "The side is ripped a little,
so I fixed it with rubber bands."

Then approached his little sister,
"Here's a dress with buttons and lace.
My grandma made it last year,"
a tender smile upon her face.

Their parents put down a box of canned food,
then quietly backed away and stood.
"We know what it's like to be without
and wanted to do whatever we could."

The preacher wore a puzzled smile
as he stared at the items lying there
and at his desk, he sat to bow his head
and speak a little prayer.

"Please bless this generous family."
He graciously asked the Lord,
"For they are the Family-in-Need
I referred to on the bulletin board."

KIND OF KIND?

To me, being "kind of kind," is like being "kind of pregnant"—not possible. You are either kind or you aren't. However, one can learn to become kind . . . if one first ensures the kindness is emanating purely from his or her heart. Kind gestures do not always equate to a kind heart. However, performing them often and with the right intentions can help you become a kinder person. It is believed that AOKs can directly improve the state of an individual's emotional well-being. Studies have shown committing acts of kindness can be beneficial to your health because a rush of euphoria and following calmness are often experienced after performing a kind act. Endorphins are said to be released in association with an AOK, a process often referred to as a "helper's high."

AS I WAKE, I GLANCE AT THE FLOOR OF MY ROOM
WHERE THE SUN'S LIGHT HAS BEGUN TO SHINE . . .
AND ASK MYSELF, "WHOSE LIFE WILL I TOUCH TODAY
. . . AND WHOSE LIFE WILL TOUCH MINE?"

THE GIFT OF TIME

This past holiday season, I received a curious greeting card in the mail. When I opened the envelope, out fell a small, unusually shaped object made from paper. I picked it up and realized it was a wonderful little bird, created through the art of origami. I opened the card and read the explanation behind this unusual little gift. The sender had noted that during the time he had spent folding the appropriate corners and angles for the enclosed present, he had thought about and prayed for the health and happiness of me and my family in the coming year. The ten or fifteen minutes it took to make my little gift, literally represented his time—time he had devoted to focusing on good wishes for me.

I was so touched by this gesture that I decided I would perform the same ritual when sending out my holiday cards next year. Instead of quickly signing and stuffing cards in envelopes, I will let the intended recipients know for those minutes, I am thinking only of them and sending best wishes for their health and well-being. Over the miles between us, I will send to them my time.

I kept that little paper bird. She sits proudly on my desk as a reminder that the greatest gift I can bestow upon anyone is the greatest gift I have been given: myself, the gift of my time. Most of us have heard the hackneyed expression: "Today is a gift—that's why they call it the present." Not only will I regift a portion of this present more often, but also I will, in turn, grant it a deeper appreciation when it is given to me.

Sympathy vs. *Empathy*

Though often used interchangeably, these words are not synonyms. The difference in the meaning of the two words is as vast as between the words *pity* and *understanding*. Although both are acts of feeling, *sympathy* represents pity or compassion, whereas *empathy* represents a deeper understanding by imagining oneself actually experiencing the plight or predicament of another, a sharing of painful feelings. They say misery loves company, but the act of sharing others' grief can literally lighten their load and ease their pain. It is a matter of saying: "I'm sorry for your pain" versus "I feel your pain."

Empathy is often derived from having gone through similar experiences and being able to draw on your own past emotions. Feeling sympathy is innate in most of us, yet feeling empathy requires taking a willful step beyond requiring a more active, emotionally involved, and non-judgmental compassion.

Before I had children, I would look at parents of unruly kids and wonder why they didn't just make their children behave. That is . . . until I was blessed with a strong-willed child. My views began to change, and I could empathize more deeply. So often, however, we encounter those who are suffering a plight that we have not endured. I stated in the introduction that a good actor, in order to appear genuine, literally places himself in the surroundings of a subject he intends to portray. We can use this same approach to become more empathetic, rather than sympathetic, to others. Instantly become an actor in your mind and take on an individual's "part." In order to be most helpful, we must try to feel what others are feeling and see things from their perspective. In other words, try to feel their pain.

You might be wondering why someone would wish to try to experience or share in another's misfortune or pain. On the surface, it would seem that doing so could make the circumstances that much harder to bear. I have learned about a Tibetan Buddhist concept called Tonglen. Tonglen entails mentally exchanging yourself for another person, thereby sharing his or her distress and your peace. The intent is to open the compassion in your heart and enhance your connection to the human condition. The effect is said to increase hope, reduce selfishness, expand loving kindness, and create more positive energy through giving and helping. The better we understand, the more we feel a person's circumstance, the more we can give, help, and love.

One of my contributors was a good friend who, sadly, recently passed away. In his youth, he had suffered a spinal injury that left one arm paralyzed. His family and friends followed his lead and rarely focused upon, or spoke about, his impediment. It was just a part of who he was and the man he had become. The only time I can remember his even mentioning his arm was when he joked to put everyone at ease, "The only thing I've found discouraging about being in a wheelchair with one good arm is that I keep going around in circles." At the time, I didn't even know whether to laugh.

Sometimes I would watch how he had mastered the art of completing life's necessary tasks, effortlessly preparing a drink or holding his daughter. We became good friends over the years; and at one time, I felt the need to experience his handicap in a more meaningful way. Unbeknown to him, I wore a makeshift sling around my arm day and night for a few days. I took a shower with my arm immobilized, I clumsily cleaned and cooked with one arm and tried to experience his dilemma personally. It was my first experience in actively attempting to convert sympathy to empathy.

Eventually, I told my friend about my inept experiences trying to "be" him, if only temporarily. He was deeply touched that I would go as far as to attempt to experience his plight. I viewed my friend in a different light from that point forward. It wasn't through sympathy, but through empathy that I learned more about his courage and determination and gained a deeper respect for him. In addition, I realized I had attained a renewed, sincere admiration for his accomplishments.

RIGHT THIS MINUTE

A while ago I waited with many other inconvenienced customers at a package delivery facility while a customer-service associate attempted to find a lost package I'd been expecting for days. As I sat quietly with the other perturbed, but patient, patrons, suddenly a woman burst through the doors. She walked directly to the counter, oblivious to the fact that there were others waiting in line and stated loudly, "I want to know the liar's name!" Surprised and dumbfounded, the employee behind the counter responded, "Ma'am?" She retorted, "The driver who said he couldn't make it up my driveway on the ice. I want his name! I made it out my driveway. I'm HERE, aren't I?" The only thing the poor stammering young man could muster in response was, "Well, it wasn't me!" Like a pit bull with a steak bone, she wouldn't give it up. She continued harping and complaining, more about the revenge she sought on this poor delivery driver than on the undelivered package. She simply wasn't going to stop until she left with what she came for, this unfortunate package-car driver's name.

As her continuous whining blended into the background of my mind, the more I thought about others—others who, right this minute, were holding a loved one's hand in the ICU, mourning the loss of someone they cared for more than life itself, or praying they wouldn't see uniformed soldiers walk up their driveway to deliver news about their child or spouse serving overseas. It had been less than a week since the horrible shooting incident in Tucson, Arizona. I bowed my head and silently thought of those who would, without hesitation, give their homes, their every possession, their every dime to have a lost package be their main concern.

I began to wonder about this woman: what makes someone lose his or her perspective to such an extent? What does it take to make people realize they need to reprioritize what they consider important? Not to diminish the inconvenience and expense this woman had obviously experienced, I tried to imagine what a package would have to contain to cause me to react in such a manner. I could imagine nothing that would be that valuable enough to me, when compared to real life. When compared to the parents of the Columbine victims, families who mourn the loss of a loved one on 9-11, service members learning to walk with a prosthetic leg or see with one eye, what could possibly be that significant that could fit in a box?

I began to wish I could offer the woman whatever magic words could change her attitude, viewpoint, and values. However, I knew it wasn't my responsibility. It would take a far greater influence than the power of a poet's words, and certainly more time than a brief meeting in a package hub to make her realize the true insignificance of her current problem compared to the genuine struggles of others. Maybe it would be necessary for her to experience great loss in her life to truly realize what is precious in her dash, what is worthy of expending such time, emotion, and effort, and what is not.

Little White Lies

While I encourage honesty and following a deal in real approach, I am a strong proponent of the little white lie when it is used in the correct context. However, we must not confuse these technical untruths with deceit. Deceit involves gossip, self-rewarding exaggeration, false flattery, and staying silent when the truth may absolve or defend another.

I don't think the use of an occasional little white lie causes harm. If not practiced habitually, in some instances, consequences are worse with the absence of a LWL. A brief example of this occurred when a friend joined the "social media" world. A few months after he had learned to post status updates and share information with lost, but never forgotten friends and family, his birthday was approaching. Speaking with him one day, he proudly announced that many of his friends and family had sent happy birthday messages to him and wished him well. In my instantly regrettable, hasty reply, I stated: "Yeah . . . a notice goes out to all of your friends a few days in advance of your birthday approaching." "Oh, uhm. I knew that," he replied. A LWL or a simple smile of acknowledgment would have been far more appropriate and sensitive in this particular situation. Why did I feel the need to give into a knee-jerk reaction to inform, rather than realize how delighted he had been that people remembered his special day? What good did it do me? What harm could it have done to execute a LWL simply by remaining silent?

However, occasionally, a little white lie can come back to haunt you. My father, with the best of intentions, told a LWL to me that he eventually came to regret. When I was a little girl, I decided to surprise him by making breakfast, consisting of eggs and toast. I was so intent on picking the eggshells out of the scrambled eggs that I didn't notice the smoke billowing from the toaster. I had inadvertently burned the toast. This wasn't the type of burned toast you could conceal with a little scraping and some thick butter but the kind of toast that would patch holes in your driveway.

Of course, being five years old, I thought whatever was lacking in quality could be made up for in presentation. So I cleverly added some freshly picked dandelion weeds from the front yard (garnish) and strategically placed them as a focal point on the opposite side of the breakfast tray to draw his attention away from the pile of carbon I was attempting to pass off as toast.

I walked into his bedroom carrying the tray and stood by his bedside waiting for—what I was hoping would be—a wonderful reaction of surprise and elation at this thoughtful and delicious gesture I'd prepared. However, to my dismay, I noticed his eyes immediately went to the toast and I was aware that my camouflage plan had failed. Afraid I'd disappointed him, I said, "Daddy, I'm sorry. I know I burned the toast." I'll never forget his reply to me, "That's okay honey. That's the way daddy likes it!"

I then watched in sheer delight as he appeared to enjoy every blackened crumb from that toast. That moment, my father made a choice. He could have shattered his little girl's heart or choose to overlook this "little thing." After all, it was just a piece of toast.

However, years later, he walked into the kitchen while my brother and I were preparing toast for Sunday breakfast. As the toast popped up, my brother began to take it out of the toaster to apply butter. I snatched it from his hand, put it back in the toaster and pushed down the lever. He said to me, "WHAT are you doing? You'll burn the toast!" To which I replied, "That's okay. That's the way daddy likes it!" To this day, I wonder how much burnt toast my father consumed on my behalf, and never said a word.

There are those who communicate using a more straightforward approach, who prefer direct truth in most occasions to the use of a little white lie. On my wedding day, for instance, attendees approached the bride (me) with wonderful, inflated, well-intentioned compliments. "Your dress is lovely." "Your hair looks beautiful." "Your veil is stunning." Then my sweet, Tennessee-grown sister-in-law approached with her beautiful, warm smile. She looked me straight in the eyes, pointed to my upper lip and exclaimed in her charming drawl, "You got sweat right thar!" (I remember wishing she had been first in line.)

How do we know when to deal in real or use a well-intended LWL? It depends on the situation, the person involved, and your understanding of his or her coping mechanisms. Perhaps it would have been better for me not to believe that the animals lying on the roadside as we drove by were just sleeping, as my father would inform me time and again. Perhaps not . . .

"Today I bent the truth to be kind, and I have no regret,
for I am far surer of what is kind than I am of what is true."
—Robert Brault

Boomerang

I've heard people use the phrase "Pay it forward." In sociology, this concept is called "generalized reciprocity." I've simplified the concept so that I, myself, can readily comprehend it and apply it to my life. Based on the simple belief "What you do comes back to you" I've dubbed it: "Boomerang."

The rationale behind the boomerang theory comes from the same basic principles of karma and kismet, that we create our own energy flow. We receive what we give. We reap what we sow. It is a belief that there is positive reaction to positive action.

I will always maintain the belief that if you do good for others, good will happen for you, too. If you think it is a coincidence, and not reciprocation, when something good happens to you, what makes you so sure?

BOOMERANG

Some people may call it karma,
but one thing I've come to know
is that we only reap in life
whatever it is we sow.

When you perform an act of kindness,
it is never unrequited
for there will always come a time
when you two are reunited.

We're all in this life together
sharing the world with one another
and so it is we help ourselves,
each time we help each other.

Like the infinite ocean waves
that steadily roll to the shore
or the predictable route
of a revolving door . . .

or the endless rhyming lyrics
of a childhood song that you sang,
your life's actions will come back to you
. . . just like a boomerang.

Greener Grass

hen I was in elementary school, a clown came to our school car-nivals. She wore a huge, billowing costume with many pockets sewn into the garment. In each pocket was a hidden surprise. Allowing us only one choice from only one pocket, she would let us select a prize. It didn't matter that the trinkets were inexpensive. It was the thrill of discovery, the unknown. Many times, after walking away inspecting my toy, another child would walk up to show me what he had chosen. No matter what it was, I distinctly remember the feeling of, "Oh, why didn't I choose that pocket. Maybe she will let me try again . . . " I couldn't shake the feelings of disappoint-ment or dispel the curiosity of what the road not taken may have offered.

It is combination of curiosity and uncertainty that breeds feelings of "the grass is always greener on the other side of the fence." So many of us consist-ently harbor the thought that there are always better alternatives "out there." Yet the desired "something" often reveals itself to be much more appealing in theory than in reality. Once we have what we think is better, we can see both sides of it, the good and the bad. It is no longer "new," and the thrill of the chase is gone. The sad part is that sometimes it takes losing what we already had for us to realize how much it truly meant to us.

I've even seen this greener-grass scenario play itself out in nature. Cows, for instance, will walk across a field of lush food to painfully stick their heads through a barbed wire fence to taste the grass on the other side. It must be better because it's not as easily attainable—it must be forbidden. If it takes more effort to get, it is more appealing and apparently more satisfying to the bovine palate. My cat will chew a hole through the corner of a bag of food, though it is the bag that contains the same food that sits in her bowl. It must be better than what she already has because it's not readily available.

To combat the greener-grass syndrome, we need to focus on the present, not the past and not the future. If we consistently believe that other "better" opportunities exist, we run the risk of squandering the opportunities in our grasp today. Next time you start to think another person has it better than you, think of how many people might be saying the same thing about you. When we focus too much on what is lacking, our eyes fail to see what is already here.

If you truly believe the grass is indeed lusher on the other side of the fence, instead of desiring a trade or change, perhaps you should learn to nurture your side. Given the proper care and appreciation, it has the potential to become every bit as verdant as what you are admiring and desiring. When you begin to appreciate more of what you have—your job, your spouse, your life's blessings—your wanderlust to relocate to greener grass, whatever it represents, will begin to subside.

I walked into the local branch of my bank the other day, where I've been banking for more than fifteen years. I was intrigued when I saw a sign announcing details of a giveaway offering free concert tickets for a performance of my favorite band. As I got closer, I read, in small, italicized print, the words: *New customers only*. I immediately felt not only disappointed, but also unappreciated. This concept was completely reversed. These gifts should be offered to those customers who had already opted to employ their services and remain reliable customers year after year, not to those who chose to join based on the enticement of a reward instead of that they preferred the reputation and services of the institution. Part of me had considered closing my account out of spite, opening a new one, and enjoying an evening attending the concert with the free tickets.

"I finally found a place where the grass is greener on the other side,
but now I'm too old to climb the fence."

—Unknown

THE NEWNESS

Why is it that newness and the not-yet-experienced are so alluring? What makes us feel that our lives will be so enhanced by abandoning the tried and true that we are willing to risk the chase for what is new? Why does it take us so long to realize that what is new isn't always better but most often provides only fleeting, temporary satisfaction?

I became the proud owner of a very intuitive breed of dog last year. As I read a book to learn more about this intelligent canine, it was suggested that I provide her with various toys to keep her mind busy and active in order to prevent boredom. The experts suggested that we keep on hand two or more sets of toys and swap them out every month to six weeks; the idea being that what my dog had been denied seeing for a period of time would become "new" once again and would thus stimulate her mind. The toys she had access to daily, had become commonplace and no longer offered excitement.

Such is the way we have allowed ourselves to become. We let the blessings currently in our lives become commonplace and, therefore, overlooked. We let familiarity breed discontent. Once the new car smells wears off, we're ready to trade. Once we have obtained one more item we assumed would satisfy us, we are seeking the next. We are misguided in believing that we climb a higher rung on the happiness ladder through each acquisition. If we can train ourselves to see the intrinsic value in what we already have, we can forever view them as good as "new." If we stop measuring our happiness around our desires, we can gain better control of our lives by gaining better control of our perceived needs.

I learned a valuable lesson from a man who did just that. My first year as a married woman, I had wanted to impress my new father-in-law with a special, thoughtful gift. I was intimidated initially by the presence of what appeared to be a strong, stern, southern man, but I soon learned he was a kindhearted, frugal gentleman, who took nothing for granted and gave sincere thanks for his blessings daily. He believed that hard work, honesty, and clean living would provide his pathway to Heaven and lived his life accordingly. During previous visits, I couldn't help but notice the paint-stained, torn coveralls he wore while tending to his large and thriving garden. A young woman at the time, I immediately viewed them as used, old, and in need of immediate replacement—a perfect opportunity to buy the perfect gift. After all, I knew he would never buy himself a new pair.

My husband and I arrived before Christmas, gifts in hand. I had located and purchased the most expensive, insulated, flame resistant, double-stitched, elastic-waist, thermal, state-of-the-art coveralls I could find. If the word *fancy* could be used as an adjective to describe a pair of coveralls that would be the word I would choose. I was anticipating the delight on his face when he opened his gift. I just knew he would agree they were exactly what he needed!

We sat on the couch and watched him open his gift. I'll never forget the quizzical look on his face when he turned and asked honestly, "What are these for?" My husband answered respectfully, "They are to replace your old worn-out pair." "Why would I want to do that?" he responded. He added, "The ones I have are just fine." I realized that he felt guilty because I had spent money on what he deemed an unnecessary expense. In this case, he didn't view new as better. What was better was what he had, what worked, and what was still perfectly functional. What he already had was just what he needed, what had served him well, and what he preferred.

How long is something considered "new"? The word *new* is undoubtedly the most overused word in advertising. *New* is enticing. *New* is inviting. *New* is fresh. *New* is innovative. *New* is followed by exclamation points!!! It is a fact that the word *new* gets attention. However, when does *new* expire? When is it technically untrue to use the word *new*? I heard a local radio station boasting the other day about their "new" station. I knew it had been around for at least a year, yet they were still availing themselves to the word because in today's world, *new* equals profit. Slight changes or enhancements, that probably would never be noticed, are implemented into products for the sole reason that manufacturers will be able to use the word *new* in its descriptive advertising.

"He who is not contented with what he has,
would not be contented with what he would like to have."

—Socrates

Live Your Dash.

ONE MORE DAY

This day . . . this precious, wonderful gift
has been bestowed upon me . . . free!
And whatever I choose to do with it
remains entirely up to me.

I could squander these given hours,
treat each task as if it's a chore
and mark this day from my calendar
like so many times before.

I could overlook the blooming flowers,
and ignore the sun's warm light
before it inevitably sets again,
turning my gift of day to night.

I could dwell upon mistakes I've made
and cry regretful tears
and live my life in the shadow of
my own anxieties and fears.

Or I could make a resolution,
before one more day has passed
that I will live it to its fullest
. . . as it if were my last.

Then I shall as I awaken
relinquish my fret and my sorrow
and accept one more day to love and laugh,
with no guarantee of tomorrow.

I shall pause to smell those flowers
and while their aroma fills my senses,
vow to bury those anxieties,
fears and defenses.

I shall drink in that sweet sunshine
as it gently warms my skin
allowing its rays to slowly blossom
my spirit from within.

I shall not pass a stranger by
without exchanging a tender smile
for this day, we shared a moment of life
. . . if only for a little while.

Each night, as I lay down my head,
only to wake again . . . I'll pray
and if I do, then I'll thank God
for giving me "One More Day."

ON
STRESS

Problem Scale

L ast year I took an unexpected trip to the emergency room after a failed attempt to descend the stairs while holding a box of holiday ornaments, which was positioned at just the right height to completely block my view of the steps beneath my feet. While I remained motionless, lying at the bottom of the staircase, I couldn't help but hear my dad's words echoing in my head: "If you're gonna be dumb, ya better be tough!"

That evening, while I sat feeling sorry for myself behind the white curtain hospitals used to eventually unveil your designated diagnosing physician, the nurse asked me to evaluate my current pain level on a scale from 1 to 10. My first thought was, *Hey, I didn't study for this test!* I hesitated to answer Nurse Ratched (affectionately nicknamed after her obvious disdain for my "Now I know why they call it a hardwood floor" joke). After all, I wanted to give an honest and concise assessment of my level of discomfort. However, as I began to evaluate the severity of my situation, I started to realize that I was not in the agony my current attitude might suggest. Sure, I was annoyed—I had so many things I had planned to accomplish that evening! But, Ms. Ratched hadn't asked me what my annoyance level was, had she? Sure, I was aggravated, but again, I wasn't being requested to peer at a cardboard aggravation scale, was I? She had asked me to assess my level of pain. When I had isolated the actual subject of her sentence, I suddenly realized that although I did require medical treatment for my injury, it wasn't painful enough to match the negative mindset I had adopted.

Always seeking self-improvement opportunities, I translated this event into how I perceive the trials and tribulations arising in my life on a regular basis. I said to myself, "Self, what if I were to calculate the severity of my problems using a hypothetical Problem Scale akin to the pain scale at the hospital?" (I think we have all done this to some extent when we see or hear of someone who is experiencing a worse circumstance than our own.) What if we literally took our problems as they arise, prior to reacting, and evaluated them on our Problem Scale?

I've read that the crux of most of our troubles lies in our reaction (or overreaction) to any given issue and not the issue itself. Furthermore, if we look solely at the core of every ordeal, without involving our reactions or emotions, we can usually immediately downgrade the issue from a perceived 10 or 9 . . . to a 5 or less—or from a Crisis to a Quandary.

I don't advise myself not to worry at all, as that would be pointless. Life does offer circumstances that will cause me to fret, cry, agonize, and sometimes panic. I cannot help my own natural emotions. However, I'm learning to differentiate those situations in which my fret and angst only add to my difficulties and, therefore, ultimately, negatively affect me.

To humor ourselves, let's imagine how we would use our Problem Scale to rate the severity levels of negative circumstances and, therefore, dictate our responses—and attitudes—toward each.

PSL = Problem Scale Level

- PSL = 10—*Crisis*—More than an ordeal. Synonyms: *Emergency, Calamity, Disaster*—May involve worry, tears, and often, high level of heart palpitations. If you can honestly categorize your issue as a #10, then feel free to give yourself a green light to proceed into the intersection of Fret & Anxiety. Most appropriate adage: "That which does not kill us, makes us stronger."

- PSL = 9—*Ordeal*—Less than a crisis, more than a dilemma. Synonyms: *Trial, Torment, Suffering*—May involve stress, tension, and a lengthy call to an advice-laden parent, family member, or high-ranking military officer (if available). Most appropriate adage: "A bend in the road is not the end of the road . . . unless you fail to make the turn."

- PSL = 8—*Dilemma*—Less than an ordeal, more than a mishap. Synonyms: *Tight Spot, Impasse*—May involve worry, sleepless nights, and/or guidance from a minimum of four good friends. Most appropriate adage: "This too shall pass."

- PSL = 7—*Mishap*—Less than a dilemma, more than a predicament. Synonyms: *Accident, Misfortune*—This type of problem may involve a local defense attorney. Most appropriate adage: "Smooth seas do not make skillful sailors."

- PSL = 6—*Predicament*—Less than a mishap, more than a quandary. Synonyms: *Mess, Pickle, Difficulty*—No clear, easy way out. Most appropriate adage: "Face the music."

- PSL = 5—*Quandary*—Less than a predicament, more than a setback. Synonyms: *Fix, Jam, Sticky Situation*—Decision(s) must be made. Often involves detailed pro vs. con list. Most appropriate adage: "The only certainty is that nothing is certain."

- PSL of 4 or less—*Setback*—Synonyms: *Temporary Impediment, Hindrance, Obstacle*—"Requires little or no reaction."

Problems with a PSL of 4 or less usually fall into the following three categories:

- That which has already happened, does not truly matter, and never will;

- that which may or may not ever happen;

• and that which has already happened, does matter, but unless you have a time machine, you are powerless to change.

Oliver Goldsmith said, "A great source of calamity lies in regret and anticipation; therefore a person is wise who thinks of the present alone, regardless of the past or future."

I would venture to guess that, if evaluated in earnest, 80 percent of my life's "problems" could rate PSL 4 or less. I've found that by practicing the art of deducting from a problem's equation, my own unnecessary fret, worry, and anxiety, I can literally reduce its rank on the scale. Gauging my reaction to the reality of each situation (by accurately assessing each using my hypothetical Problem Scale) allows me to respond more appropriately.

So next time life presents an opportunity for you to react with the three IMs: IMpatiently, IMpulsively, and IMpetuously, try measuring the issue on your Problem Scale. It takes a combination of self-awareness and truth, but it may help you cope and react more positively to negative situations. You'll find a large amount of what you brand "problems" wouldn't qualify as such if they were overlooked, instead of labeled.

Morning Mantra

Have you ever been awoken in the morning by a song on the radio, and it would not stop playing inside your head all day? You find yourself humming the melody while you commute to work. You sing the lyrics under your breath. The song may stay with you all day and even the day after. Why? Because when you awoke that morning, your mind was clear and free from the responsibilities the day would soon cast upon you. It was in the middle of that fuzzy haze between sleep and wakefulness. Your mind was a clean slate, and that song seized and saturated those untapped brain cells with hypnotic potency. I've read that it is more beneficial to eat fruit in the morning because your stomach is empty, and therefore, will absorb the nutrients more efficiently. Same theory applies; it just makes sense.

Using those suggestions, why not use that special time to focus on some simple, positive messages that will help you stay content, in control, and happy throughout your day? I'm referring to the audible repetition of a personal morning mantra. I've written a morning mantra for myself, but you could write anything you feel would give you the confidence, fortitude, and emotional stability to face whatever challenges each new day may bring. Alter your mantra weekly, daily, or whatever fits your schedule and circumstances. I've used mine for months because it works for me. I also repeat it in the morning about fifteen minutes BC (before coffee), as that is when my brain has the capabilities similar to that of a slow slug. It is the optimum time to take advantage of my brain cells before they begin the phenomena of multitasking.

I began the morning mantra routine because often I would wake with positive feelings about the day that would lie ahead. However, as soon as I would get stuck in traffic, get to work, check my e-mail and voice mail, and be bombarded by the black hole otherwise known as my to-do list, my wonderfully enlightened mood would plummet faster than a heavy kid on a see-saw. I wanted to devise a method to revert to that positive, wake-up-happy, nothing-is-wrong feeling I had experienced just hours before.

To assist in re-creating and maintaining those positive feelings, I created a morning mantra, and I highly suggest you do the same. Mine, of course, rhymes, because that's what I do. Your mantra doesn't have to rhyme, but some form of repetitiveness, uniformity, or alliteration is recommended if you wish to memorize it for easy recollection.

Your mantra might serve several different purposes. Mine is solely to maintain (or insert) a positive attitude during the day. Yours may be to reaffirm specific beliefs, help you to control your reactions to negative events, or assist you in maintaining peace of mind during the happenings, routine or unexpected, that occur during the course of a day.

Live Your Dash.

I WILL (MANTRA)

I will choose how this day goes
no matter what may come my way.
I can only live this time one time;
the minutes, the hours, the day.

I will smile through adversity,
let malice be ignored,
and release the spite and pettiness
that today, won't be restored.

I will heed constructive views,
though they may appear as flak
and force unkind deeds and insults
to roll right off my back.

I will complete Acts of Kindness
in my own special style
not just for the benefit of others,
but because they make me smile.

My heart and soul are now content;
life's blessings overflow
and I will be the only one to blame
if I let these feelings go.

On-Call

He was very thin and equally as frail. His long, pale fingers grasped the handset of the cordless phone as he lay there hour after hour impatiently awaiting his own permanent departure. He was dying, yet he was still on-call.

My father was neither a paramedic nor a firefighter. He was neither a heart surgeon nor an obstetrician awaiting a frantic call from a soon-to-be mother. Yet, he held that telephone in his fragile hand as if it represented a lifeline connecting him to all that he would leave behind. Having every intention of turning the ringer off, I tried to gently remove the phone from his grasp while he slept peacefully. He awoke abruptly and angrily grabbed the phone back from my hand. I stood in stunned silence. He was unable to speak without extreme exertion, walk unattended, eat solid foods, or see without double vision; and yet, he held onto this item as if it were a handful of pure gold.

I asked him, humbly, what reasons he could possibly have under the circumstances, for wanting the phone in his hand at all times. He answered with four simple words: "Someone might need me."

My father was always on-call for his family and friends, literally. I know of no one who had requested his help, guidance, or assistance, who had not received an immediate response. He lived every hour as if he were anticipating some level of calamity. It was apparent to anyone who met him that he was often physically tense and hurried. Though he enjoyed his life and his family immeasurably, the self-induced stress he experienced, at times, shone through his cheerful green eyes.

And though the reliable safety net he had constructed for my life was always there for me to freefall into, I didn't realize until that net was gone how much it hurt to hit the ground. Though his intentions were sincere and appreciated, I've realized that his practice of catching me before I would fall prevented me from learning how to prevent the fall in the first place.

In the years since his death, I realized that subconsciously I had followed the same pattern by putting up a secure safety net for my loved ones, living my life on-call, anticipating their need for me through every hour of every day. For many years, I never spent a peaceful moment because of a nagging sensation that things were to change in a moment's notice. I could not take a drive, a shower, or spend one hour at work with complete clarity and focus, as I was always prepared to jump at any possible request or requirement. That constant burning sensation that "someone might need me" could not be extinguished.

That is, until I realized I was suffering from on-call syndrome. Through personal observation, I had recognized that I was constantly anticipating misfortune that I believed would require my (and only my) assistance to rectify. I had built my relationships upon the premise that I would be available in an instant to assist and support. I had convinced myself that I, myself, was the only missing piece to a puzzle my family's and friends' lives might depend upon solving. It seems I was readily available upon request to everyone in my life, except me. Technology had even made the situation more severe. With cell phones, texting, and e-mail, today the demands of others are shot from different directions like arrows aiming at their target: your time.

I simply had to learn how to combine being dependable—which meant, in my mind, being instantaneously available for my children, spouse, friends, and bosses—with being available to myself, for myself. Living on-call meant my time was first given to others and what was left over, if anything, could then be given without guilt to me. In order to obtain inner peace, I had to discover and maintain a healthy degree of selfishness.

In the years before his illness, my brothers and I would chide my bachelor father about the contents in his refrigerator. We had gone so far as to create an imaginary "line" at the halfway point on the top shelf. Following the definition of "displacement" I recall from chemistry class, (a reaction in which an atom or molecule replaces another in a compound) the incoming fresh perishables would push the items with more seniority "behind the line" and toward the back. No one who visited often had the bravery to venture into this forbidden zone for sustenance, no matter how strong his or her hunger pangs.

When we live on-call, we train ourselves to put our own needs behind the line, sacrificing what we require and desire in order to fulfill the constant incoming needs of others.

Is this what happens to your needs? Do the requirements and demands of your boss, your spouse, your children, and others push what you need for yourself "behind the line," where they are ignored and left unattended? A selfless life of putting your needs behind all others is admirable and unquestionably a quality one seeks to find in a "good" parent, friend, spouse, or employee. However, failing to put our own needs foremost is an unhealthy practice and often leads to undue stress. In addition, because we live our days on-call, we assume others will do the same for us. When they don't, though we may convince ourselves it doesn't matter, resentment will follow. Their hurtful lack of reciprocity will fester and eventually morph itself into additional stress. Denying yourself to tend to the needs of others first can prove to be a great stress inducer.

Though often not held accountable, stress can lead to headaches, digestive problems, and a slew of additional health disorders. Because self-sacrifice leads to stress, the end result is greater sacrifice than you'd anticipated investing. Finding a degree of healthy selfishness will likely result in less physical and psychological stress and, thus, a healthier, happier you.

It makes sense that when you feel happier, more positive and less stressed, you can give more to others. The quantity of yourself that you give may be reduced, but the quality of what you give will increase twofold. So, by reaching your own full potential, you actually increase the value of what you have to offer others. If you are the best you can be, then you give others the best of you. You owe it to yourself. You owe it to them.

There is a reason airline attendants request that, in an emergency, you put on your own oxygen mask first before helping children with theirs. By putting in place a healthy selfishness, and taking care of your own needs before you attend to the needs of another, you ensure that you have the best of yourself to give.

I am not suggesting any parent, friend, spouse, or employee be unresponsive or undependable. What I am offering is that by putting yourself first, you will be more capable and more willing to satisfy their requirements and demands of your time, energy, and life. Uncovering a healthy degree of selfishness can help give you freedom—freedom from the on-call syndrome—from the judgment and guilt from your own conscience. I've read that a mother is someone who, when she finds there are only three pieces of pie for four people, will quickly announce that she never did care for pie. Admirable, but you don't have to be the world's mother. Matter to yourself.

Steve Roland Prefontaine said, "To give anything less than your best is to sacrifice the gift."

You can turn off the on-call button in your mind by ceasing to continually anticipate negative events that may never happen and by realizing that you cannot live your hours in ready mode for others. By putting the needs in your dash first, you make yourself the best you can be, and the best is, therefore, all you will have to give others.

The Noise of Life

Though the lightning and thunder had passed our home, remnants of the storm's dark clouds lingered, resulting in a sudden loss of electricity. We each froze at our respective locations throughout the house, realizing that the task we were in the middle of performing had been halted and for how long, no one could know. The room became dark, so I stood and walked purposefully down the stairs, using the light from my cell phone to guide my way. At the bottom of the staircase, my anxious teenage daughter greeted me. She was repeatedly flipping the light switch as she entered each room, as if the result would be different in the dining room from what it had been in her previous failed attempt in the hallway. The thought hit me that I should have taken her camping more often.

I calmly began to search for a lighter, candles, and the flashlight while listening to her express disappointment that we, as a family, were not prepared as well as we should be for situations "like this." A creature of habit myself, I too unsuccessfully flipped the light switch for the umpteenth time as, through the darkness, I followed my instincts and located my fully charged laptop. I opened the screen, and it began to shine like a beacon in the night, guiding me to its brightly lit keyboard. I could have sworn I heard angelic music playing in the background and caught a brief glimpse of a golden halo surrounding it as it sat proudly on the desk . . . as if somehow it knew it was the only appliance currently operational in the household.

I quietly sat in my chair and began typing in the dark. The more I typed, the more I contemplated the current situation. I began to experience a lengthy consciousness of sorts as I realized how dependent I had let myself become on the little luxuries of life, those I had taken for granted every day. Except for the clicking of the keys on the keyboard, I could hear nothing. In the darkness, I could feel the deafening silence almost beckoning me, challenging me to mentally reach inside. With the absence of the monotonous sounds of the television, I stared blankly at the burning wick of the candle flame. As I stared, I felt more and more compelled to reach . . . deep inside . . . to the place where my thoughts and memories are safely housed and protected. New and insightful ideas began to blossom and faded memories paraded themselves through my mind. My typing skills were set at warp speed as the computer screen rapidly displayed, letter by letter, word by word, that which my mind was willingly and freely presenting to me . . . as if it had been waiting for the chance.

I paused momentarily and walked to the window in order to peer out into the total darkness. In the stillness of the night, I tried to recall the last time I had sat in silence, with the company of only myself. I was, initially, uneasy with this situation. It was, after all, unfamiliar territory. It was a sudden, unexpected, temporary marriage of myself to my surroundings. It was a type of compulsory meditation.

I realized with sadness that my world, that which surrounds me every day, is simply filled with too much noise . . . the noise of life. Accompanying this silence, after an initial adjustment period, came a subtle calmness followed quickly by a renewed ability to focus. I asked myself how I had let my world become so crowded with details and mayhem that I no longer sought, or experienced, silent moments? More importantly, had I forgotten how?

Had I become so dependent on the noise of life, that I had forgotten how to clear and hear my own thoughts? Would I, could I, take my mind back to the days before children boisterously ran through my home, before the Internet, before cell phones and fax machines when the sun's rays cast across a mystery novel would suffice as a natural stress reliever? Then, I asked myself honestly: "How long can you endure the silence?"

Startled and surprisingly dismayed, I jumped as the electricity rudely interrupted my quiet and surged through the house providing sustenance to light bulbs and electrical appliances. The power had returned, and with it, the ultimate nemesis of true peace and tranquility—technology. I ruefully bade farewell to the quiet moments I'd spent that evening . . . with me.

Though we had lost electricity at times before that evening, that particular occurrence will be the one I will remember most because it brought a whole new level of awareness into my life. Partly because those hours put a permanent kink in an ever-increasing chain of chaos by making me realize I need to seek more opportunities for moments of silence. I need to make more time to spend with me. I had allowed silence and serenity to slowly escape from my life, leaving a void I had not recognized, yet one that needed to be filled. I had unknowingly let my "self" become lost, twisted and tangled in the complexities of life like a feather in a windstorm.

SILENCE ITSELF IS A SEAMLESS CONDUIT

THROUGH WHICH WE ARE ABLE TO,

WITHOUT INTERRUPTION, REACH THOSE

THOUGHTS, IDEAS AND MEMORIES

THAT ARE RELENTLESSLY SUPPRESSED BY THE NOISE . . .

THE NOISE OF LIFE.

Loneliness vs. Solitude

Though often used interchangeably, the two words are quite unique in definition. *Solitude* is "the act of finding peace while being alone." *Loneliness* is "suffering pain while being alone." Though *solitude* may mean "loneliness" to some, you can be lonely without experiencing solitude, like when you feel lonely in a crowd. Solitude, not loneliness, is often elusive. Unlike loneliness, it should be planned, anticipated, sought after, and desired. You are your only company in solitude, and it is the most effective way, through reflection, introspect, and personal growth to truly get to know who you really are.

The moment you realize that being alone doesn't mean being lonely, you can draw strength and benefit from solitude. Quiet moments offer opportunities to listen instead of hear. They provide a calmness that can replenish, renew, and regenerate. Silencing the chatter makes more room in your head for free-roaming thoughts. Inner peace stems from inward quietness. After spending times of solitude, you will often emerge with new perspectives and a more positive attitude. You will have succeeded in cultivating an everlasting friendship—the one you have with yourself.

CAN YOU SIT IN SILENCE?

CAN YOU FIND A SILENT PLACE?

IN YOUR WORLD OF CONSTANT CHAOS,

DOES THERE EXIST SUCH A SPACE?

Simple City

My oldest brother used to say, during the more harried period of his life, that he would like to take his brain out and rinse it. I've often felt, theoretically at least, that I could do that very thing; just rinse away the unnecessary clutter and the non-essential data of life in order to see more clearly, make more room, simplify. I had allowed the insignificant to weigh so heavily on my mind, I was surprised the airlines didn't charge me extra on my last flight for carrying so much emotional baggage on board.

I think I've established by now that I believe the inconsequentialities of life in this century can, at times, cause a person to go temporarily berserk. If I haven't, I've been remiss. However, in reality, it is not life itself causing our chaos. Life hasn't changed, only its surroundings have. It is the way we choose to react to those surroundings that determine their direct effect on our quality of life. Today, we need to turn our attention to focus on the demands and burdens that swallow life whole. Living is getting lost somewhere in the swirling vortex of responsibilities and insignificant matters that so often consume our time. Yet, the steps on the ladder of superficial success entice us to keep climbing. Like an escalator, the steps continue to reappear, replacing themselves endlessly, ensuring that the climb continues.

It's often been suggested that we should separate our needs from our wants, and after we realize our needs are actually met, voila!—instant life satisfaction! However, as most of us have discovered, it's just not that easy. If you made a list of your needs and your wants in order to distinguished the two and, therefore, live happily ever after, your needs would list three things:

Food, Water, Shelter. Naturally, with such a small number of items in the "Needs" column, the "Wants" column would eventually trickle over into it . . . and (just to even things out a little) we would allow them to stay. After all, we want everything we need, but we don't need everything we want. When you quiet the unnecessary, you give the necessary the opportunity to be heard. It was when I found myself feeling worry and sadness over the loss of something that was never alive, I knew it was time for a change.

How do we escape from the spinning currents of this vortex? The answer is to pack up and leave. I don't mean to physically pack your suitcases and buy a plane ticket. I am referring to mentally packing up only that which you require and relocating to another city—Simple City (simplicity). However, mentally relocating to Simple City is easier said than done. It requires a commitment to eliminate the clutter in your life and get rid of many of the things you have and do, so that you can free more of your time to spend with people you love and doing things you love. The concept is easy to understand: the simpler your life becomes, the more control you will have over it. As you begin to emerge from past limitations and discover the flexible boundaries of Simple City, the feelings of freedom will expand to other areas of your life. Simple living isn't about deprivation; it's about enrichment.

THE PROCESS OF ELIMINATION

Do you love it, do you use it, and does it make you feel good to see it? Does this thing make your life easier or more comfortable? If you answer no, let it go. Most people were not aware of the profession of "professional organizer" ten years ago, nor were there reality shows on TV that focused on the lives of those who suffer from a condition now known as "hoarding." There were no advertisements for "space bags" to flatten and store items just to make room for more. Trying to live an uncluttered life today is comparable to rowing a small boat against the tide, against the wind, and toward a colossal tidal wave. Though you set out with good intentions and a strong will to reach your destination, the combination of a continuous influx of outside influences eventually dissolves your resolve, and you unwillingly surrender to the direction of the tide.

In the interest of full disclosure, my desire for simplicity in the physical sense stemmed from a breathing disorder. In the pursuit of a healthier life, "things" began to represent little more to me than dust collectors, the accumulation of which had the potential to affect my quality of life. However, as I soon discovered, the more items I had amassed through the years, the more cost, time, money, and energy I was forced to invest and the less room I had left to devote to life. It's as though I had been initially blessed with a clear vision to see forward, but I had slowly, unintentionally, blocked my view in every direction with things. The more I eliminated, the clearer my view was and the more freedom, and peace, became mine. I immediately began to feel lighter, less encumbered, and more in control. I'd began the process of elimination, both physically and mentally. I realized possessions had begun to constrict and prevent my mind's freedom and affect my lightness for life.

The first step in the process was to remove what wasn't important, necessary, or didn't make me smile. This included not only tangible items, but also commitments of my time and an honest evaluation of the excess time I'd spent using communication technology. I had become a technological addict, and my phone and computer were my enablers. A useful piece of advice is that you should become your own editor. "Edit" each room, drawer, and closet in your home. Edit your to-do list, your commitments to others and unnecessary deadlines. Concentrate on only the important, the core, the necessary . . . the minimum required. When you realize that having too much and doing too much will in turn edit the quality of your life, you'll find it is an easy decision to make.

ENOUGH ALREADY

Enough: sufficient, adequate, as much as necessary. The entire act and process of simplifying your life can be based entirely upon this word. The first time you absorb its intent and realize that you have enough, the more you can begin the process of elimination on the more than enough.

Superfluous: not only a fun word to pronounce, but one that hosts a significant definition as well. Extra, redundant, unnecessary, excessive, surplus . . . all synonyms of the profound, four-syllable utterance, superfluous. The physical stuff we accumulate is not just physical. It clouds our judgment, our ability to see clearly through the density of life and just be. With each piece of "stuff" we acquire, comes a responsibility, another knot tied into the ropes that bind our life's freedom. Life itself is weightless, buoyant, and without boundaries. Stuff, items, and belongings eventually prove to be effective, invisible anchors attaching our free awareness to that which is stationary.

If your vision of life has slowly become obscured, though you may never wish to reach minimalist status, why not try packing up your essentials and consider becoming a permanent resident of Simple City?

INNER/OUTER PEACE

Recording artist Suzie Bogus once sang in one of her songs: "Wherever you go, it's bound to rain." To me, that always translated into the fact that I couldn't run away from my problems. Oh, I could lounge on a tropical beach somewhere and recline with a cold, umbrella-clad drink in my hand, but I would soon be consumed, bombarded, by my thoughts, worries, resentments, and regrets. I learned quickly that inner peace and outer peace were intertwined, and I could not fully obtain one, without having mastered the other. Relaxation was experienced only momentarily. I had the equation in reverse. I was trying to achieve inner peace through outer peace, setting myself up for eventual failure. If peace was to be truly attained, it was clear I would have to work from the inside, out.

> "Peace: It does not mean to be in a place where
> there is no noise, trouble or hard work.
> It means to be in the midst of those things and
> still be calm in your heart."
>
> —Anonymous

I realized that I had let my mind become so filled with the pettiness in life, peace had no room to enter. I compared it to the pie-chart graph that shows the full system capacity on my computer's hard drive. It is divided into sections including unused programs and idle, useless downloaded files that offer nothing valuable or positive, just take up space. When I'd considered how much of my "chart" was attributed to unnecessary worry and angst and importance placed on unimportant matters, I was almost filled to capacity. The petty things, the junk mail, the deadlines, the accumulation of the irrelevant, were occupying far too much space within me, within my life.

One of the underlying themes of the dash poems, in summary, is that we shouldn't spend precious minutes on that which doesn't really matter. Those who don't "get" this philosophy are those who have trouble discerning what matters and what doesn't. "Don't sweat the petty stuff." Most of us have heard it. Most of us believe it. Yet, we seem to lose perspective in the moment. We forget the philosophy entirely during our involvement in stressful situations. We too hastily dismiss the principle when it doesn't serve our current purpose.

It's as easy as stopping to ask yourself three brief questions when you can feel anger, worry, and frustration begin to rise up within you: Does it truly matter now? Will it truly matter later? Is it worth it? If you answer yes, more than no, to these questions during times of perceived worry and pressure, you need to seriously consider a shift in perspective. But how?

Tolerance. Mastering the ability to be tolerant is a vital step in eliminating stress, attaining inner peace, and learning how not to sweat the petty stuff. We all have limits to that which we can accept before necessitating a response. The art of being tolerant requires learning how to voluntarily push beyond those limits without feeling a need to respond, and at some point, without a second thought. The idea can be likened to the act of pouring a drink from a soda can into a glass. You pour until the liquid nears the top, become impatient and continue to pour just a tad more. That small addition causes the drink to spill over the top. The glass has reached its tolerance limit and responded.

Many speak of teaching tolerance, but to truly grasp the concept, we can only teach ourselves. If we were all born with a tolerance gene, hatred and prejudice would dissipate as fast as respect would rise. The practice of tolerance can annihilate anger, impatience, irritation, and frustration. It can be the tool you learn to rely on most to help you stop putting so much emphasis, and wasting too much precious time, on the minor, petty things in life. Tolerance can be infused into every aspect of your life. Tolerance involves granting everyone the benefit of the doubt and being anti-reactionary. When you practice immediate tolerance (in lieu of after-the-fact tolerance), the discourteous drivers, the medicine bottles that are difficult to open, the elusive parking spot, will begin to represent less importance in your day, in your dash. It will soon appear to you that your life is running smoother, more peacefully, though it is not life that has changed, but you.

Tolerance is patience. Tolerance is acceptance. Tolerance is belief in the reality that you don't always have to be right. Based on unique life experiences, diverse backgrounds, and religious and political beliefs, it's amazing we agree on anything—ever. You can't change much of what irks or disagrees with you during your lifetime. The only practical, healthy strategy is to learn to accept what is by respecting others' viewpoints and beliefs. When your heart and mind tell you something is the way it should be, let it be that way, for you. If others do not see it your way, respect that their views are founded from their own experiences, realities, and consciences. "The Dash" poem speaks of treating each other with respect. When one's opinion, religion, or political party differs from yours, do not automatically assume it is "wrong." Remaining firm in your own convictions doesn't mean disrespect must permeate the process. Once you swap the desire to impose change with the act of acceptance, the door to tolerance remains open.

Have you ever argued so strongly about an incident that you wished life had an instant-reply button so that you could prove yourself right? So often a replay, however, would prove just the opposite. Through our need to be correct, we often subconsciously review the past differently in our minds and unintentionally distort the facts. It takes many occurrences of humbly being proven incorrect to realize that we are not always right. In addition, two people can encounter the exact same incident and perceive it entirely differently. Maturity teaches us it is far less complicated and peace sustaining to learn to swallow your pride and agree to disagree.

No matter how strongly you believe you're right,

never declare it so strong . . .

as to cause you embarrassment, when and if,

you're eventually proven wrong.

None of us are a deity. We are all born astonishingly imperfect with countless flaws and deficiencies. No one is birthed with a gavel in his or her hand and immediately granted the right to judge others. So why do so many of us appear to thrive on criticizing others or follow along with other critics instead of expressing discontent and leaving the room, rebutting the statements, or changing the subject?

If you are a person who has appointed yourself a judge or know others who have, honestly answer these questions before judgment is again decreed:

- What makes you, or them, qualified for such a position?

- Do you, do they, judge yourself or themselves, first?

- Does belittling others make you, or them, rise up on an invisible social scale?

- Do you, or they, believe that demeaning others will make your, or their, own light shine brighter?

- Does this unworthy habit stem from haughty confidence or lack thereof?

Offer the benefit of the doubt prior to offering criticism and disparagement by reflecting upon the wise saying: Those who judge don't matter, and those who matter, don't judge.

ON
LIFE

The "Me's"

I am not the same me I was. I never will be. Over the years, each individual me has morphed into the next, and there is no way of knowing how many me's remain to be experienced. There was the teenage me, the corporate me, the single me, the married me, the overweight me, the mommy me, the author me, and the list goes on. It's as though each me had its own lifetime, yet all of them together make up the life of the me I am today. I often ask myself if the me I am today is the me I had hoped to become when I was the me I was then. Confused?

Since our beliefs, tastes, visions, likes, and dislikes change so dramatically as we age, in hindsight sometimes it feels as though we were different people throughout the stages of our lives. What is important to me today wasn't important to me then. What I feed me today wasn't what I fed me then. What I do for a living to support me now isn't what I did to support me then. Some believe fate and destiny determine the me you are at any given time. Others believe you create your own reality through choices. Whether by fate or by choice, the timing of the combination of surroundings, age, knowledge, and maturity combine to create each individual me.

How many times have you looked back on something you did, said, or wore and thought: WHAT was I thinking? The mindset of the me you were then found it perfectly acceptable and appropriate; however, the me you are today may find it unacceptable or even deplorable. People from whom you are estranged today may have been the closest of friends of a me from the past, and those closest in your life now may be people a previous me wouldn't have considered befriending.

The secret is not in comparing, criticizing, or ruing the actions of our me's but to understand that each me is an important, individual contributor. Each me brings forth invaluable, previously unlived experiences, views, life lessons, sights, sounds, skills, memories, and emotions. Realize that each me is a vital donor to its successor. Though you may wish you could bypass certain stages—the grieving me, the angry me, the confused me—each phase will cumulatively merge in succession with the next. Like a snowball rolling down a hill, we gather, we retain, we grow as we continue the journey. My grandmother was old (as most grandmothers tend to be), and I never knew her as anything else. I never knew the young, vibrant me she once was. In fact, until I grew older, I had never considered that her younger me ever existed. However, the me she was during my lifetime represented an important part of the me I am today.

Is the me you are today the me you had planned to be, hoped to be, dreamed of being? Do you allow your reaction to events in your life to alter the me you still have the potential to become? When you accept that you cannot travel back to any me you once were or forward to any me you will eventually become, you realize that your only option is to make the me you are today the best it can be. Think about what steps need be taken to transform you into the me you know you can be.

BETTER THAN YESTERDAY

If changing into a better me is an overwhelming thought for you, consider taking small but significant steps one day at a time. Viewing all the changes you'd like to implement at once can be overwhelming and the worst type of de-motivator. It is a habit that provides more discouragement than encouragement and often dampens your spirit before you are able to begin. If you know you were a better person today than you were just yesterday and the same applies to the day prior, then you are on the right path to becoming the best me possible and that is all you should ask of yourself. Was I a better person today than I was yesterday? Your actions, your words, and your attitude are the only things that can validate a yes answer to that question.

When you ask yourself that question, focus only on this day that has passed. What you did yesterday is over, and all the money in the world cannot rectify blunders or erase your mistakes. Your actions of tomorrow are yet to be unveiled. An unknown author wrote, "We have no stake in tomorrow, for it is yet to be born." There is no guarantee of tomorrow; therefore, we should accept the reality that today is all that we need now. An old saying about a sign hanging in a luncheonette epitomizes this concept: Free Lunch Tomorrow! The restaurant owner would hang the same sign every day knowing that tomorrow is always forthcoming. When tomorrow becomes a reality, it is considered today.

A unique view of the "me" concept is to imagine having had the tools along the journey that would have enabled you to communicate with today's me. Does that idea make you immediately ponder things you may have done differently or another route your life may have taken? Does it make you wonder in what ways you could have benefited from your experiences to avoid the pitfalls and errors you were undoubtedly certain to make? If you were granted the opportunity to send a letter to your younger me's, what may it have contained?

Live Your Dash.

DEAR ME,

I've heard it said, "If I knew then . . .
everything that I know now . . . "
But we are taught at a proven pace
that time . . . and life . . . will both allow.

I could have saved a lot of time
and saved myself a lot of pain,
if I could have only been a student
for me, myself, to train.

So many changes I would make
from the lessons I'd convey,
to make the person who I used to be
more like who I am today.

Both classrooms and teachers
are life . . . love . . . and fate.
And I hope to have far more to learn
before I "graduate."

If there had been a way to teach myself
to live a better life, instead,
I would have written "me" a letter
and this is how it might have read:

Dear Me,

Make the most of every moment.
Be your own shining star.
Though you may not be
where you want to be,
it's still where you are . . .

Laugh much and laugh often.
Life is supposed to be fun.
Find humor in most everything
that can be said, heard or done.

In love, not everyone is perfect,
nor can you make them so.
If you can't accept them as they are,
then you need to let them go.

Have in place, a "Plan B"
so you won't ever be caught
unequipped for what might happen
and unprepared for what might not.

Be an open-minded person;
success comes from give and take.
Remain as flexible as the willow
that bends, so it won't break.

There are reasons every person
is the person they've become.
Search for the good. (Though it might
take more effort with some.)

Recognize a sign that indicates
you may be slightly "out of touch,"
is when you realize you are worrying
that you worry too much.

Don't be a slave to monotony;
to routine, be but a guest.
Those who welcome change with open arms
know it's usually for the best.

Cultivate relationships;
do not take things for granted.
Don't anticipate roses
just because seeds were planted.

Always double check for accuracy,
heeding the carpenter's advice:
"You will only have to saw once . . .
if you will measure twice."

Be yourself. Don't try to impress,
by being something that you're not.
And in turn, love others for what they are
and not for what they've got.

Don't put up defenses,
even when you've gotten hurt.
Don't be more afraid . . .
just be more alert!

Learn to follow your instincts,
more than your ambitions
by listening to your heart
and to your own intuitions.

Though it hurts, live through your pain
and experience your sorrow.
Putting off the grief or anguish
only leaves it for tomorrow.

If you hold on to resentment,
you'll hold it as long as you live.
And the only way to release it,
is to accept . . . and to forgive.

Do not expect to be acknowledged
for everything you say and do.
When you do good things for others,
good things will happen for you, too.

If your conscience is in doubt,
the answer becomes clearer
when you look honestly into the eyes
reflected in your mirror.

Do not encroach on others' privacy,
and let them not intrude on yours.
Focus only on what happens
behind your OWN closed doors.

Walk in someone else's shoes.
Do what your heart knows is right.
Be compassionate to those in need
and empathetic to their plight.

Focus on the positive,
even in times of despair.
Count all of your blessings.
You will find them everywhere.

Don't be always in a hurry.
Decelerate your haste.
Take time to realize your senses . . .
to see . . . to touch . . . to taste.

Treat everyone with kindness.
Wear a smile upon your face.
Offer your shoulder to catch tears,
and your arms to embrace.

And now I'll close this letter,
though I've so much more to share.
I cannot send these lessons to a youth
that is no longer there.

Sealed in an envelope, will be this note
I only wish I could have read
when I had lived but sixteen years
and had so many more, ahead.

Automatic Pilot

Automatic Pilot: a navigation device, such as on an aircraft, that when manually activated, will maintain a preset course, thereby releasing the operator from necessary, but mundane or routine actions. So many of us, without realizing it, "flip the switch" over to automatic pilot far too often as we navigate through life's journey. Most of us don't even realize we are doing it as we move through our days like robots, subconsciously treating life as no more than a purchase of death on an installment plan.

Those who use their brain's automatic pilot feature often are content to just let life happen, allowing the world to decide their actions. They have often mastered the art of eating without tasting. They can hear, but they do not listen. They see, yet they have no vision. They touch, but they don't feel. They have a life, but they are not living.

Many prefer to climb aboard a mental catamaran and glide safely over the whitecaps on the waves of life, allowing themselves to slice through the surface just enough to stay safely afloat. They never grant themselves the opportunity to discover what might exist beneath the surface. With mounting family and job responsibilities, they may continue to drift through an uninspired life for years, comfortable and without much chance of variance. They silently yearn for change but are hesitant to take the steps necessary, because they find an underlying security and an invisible layer of comfort in this lackluster strategy for living their dash.

Of course, some of what we do each day must naturally fall under the "autopilot" category. If we had to contemplate every decision we faced daily, we would spend too much time just making decisions. Much of what we do requires a degree of automaticity, such as tying a shoelace, or brushing our teeth. So, how do we eliminate the autopilot syndrome? How do we regain and maintain balance and a sense that we are indeed the captain at the helm, steering the ship of our life? The answer, as always, is to deal in real.

You can take back the wheel and change direction simply by ceasing to deny that you are indeed in control of the route, the speed, and the destination. You are the pilot. You are the captain. You are at the helm. Through honest reflection, you will soon realize that the power you have used to create the life you are currently living is the same power you can rely upon to create the life you'd rather be living. You need to pay attention. You need to pay attention to you.

Karma, kismet, and the law of attraction . . . they are all fascinating reading and wonderful, positive approaches to life. Waiting on karma, however, to pay the dividends you may be due or depending on the law of attraction to change the direction of your life does not deal in real. Many philosophers, dreamers, and inspirational gurus claim that you can change your life by creating your own reality. However, the definition of *reality* is, "the world or state of things as they actually exist." Sure, I'd like to make my own reality mimic Disney World, but the state of things as they actually exist prohibit me from doing so. By suggesting that you must create your own reality, these concepts are, in essence, saying that you should create a false reality—which is, itself, an oxymoron—and learn to live comfortably in a state of denial. If you were, however, to deal in real, you could focus on making your own happiness, accepting and proceeding with an "it is what it is" approach, and learning to be content inside your real reality. Many have written that if you can "envision a success," you can make it happen. Deal in real. I can envision myself a size six, but unless I put down the cheesecake, it's not happening. Change what you can. Accept what you can't. And move on. You are often your biggest obstacle. Move over . . . don't stand in your own way.

FRESH FISH

It's well known that Japanese cuisine highlights the taste of fresh fish. Unfortunately, fresh fish have not been as plentiful in the waters close to Japan as they were decades ago. Therefore, in order to adapt to their present circumstances, new fishing boats were built to be bigger, and boats in existence were customized so that they could venture farther out to sea. However, the downside was that the farther each excursion took, the longer it took to bring the fish to back to port. Naturally, the longer the trip, the less fresh the haul of fish. The less fresh the fish, the less Japanese eaters liked the taste.

Ingeniously, in an effort to solve this problem, fishing companies began installing on-board freezers for their boats. Freezers allowed them to go out farther in search of fish, because after catching the fish, they would freeze them at sea, hoping to immediately preserve their freshness. The unforeseen result was that the Japanese could distinguish the taste between "fresh" fish and "freshly frozen" fish. They did not respond favorably, and fishermen's profits did not rise as much as they'd anticipated.

The next step was for the fishing companies to install fish tanks. They would catch the fish and store them in freshwater tanks. But, they crammed the tanks so full of previously active fish that the fish ran out of room to thrash and swim. They were alive, but virtually motionless. This, eventually, had an effect on the "fresh" fish taste as well, as their immobility would cause staleness that the trained Japanese palate could immediately discern. They preferred the lively taste of freshly caught fish, not frozen, not stale.

The answer to the fishing companies' dilemma was to add another ingredient to the fish tanks . . . a small, but very alive, shark. The fish were now challenged. They were compelled to move in order to ensure their own survival. A small percentage of the fish eventually become victims of the hungry shark's teeth, but they were considered collateral damage, as the eventual outcome was that a majority of the fish arrived in a lively, fresh state.

Some of us are living in still waters: tired, dull, and monotonous. What we need is a "shark" to keep us motivated, inspired, and to get us moving once again. Sharks can be new challenges, hobbies, or passions that keep our minds active and alert. Examine various ways in which you can add a shark to different aspects of your dash. Change your driving route to work, begin listening to a different type of music, visit new restaurants. Polish what has become lackluster; jar your own consciousness. Even small changes have the ability to awaken your awareness once again.

Live Life in Person

If you have resigned yourself to believing that the best years of your life have gone by, you are not living life in person. Each day you wake up on the right side of the soil, you owe it to yourself to live that day to its fullest. Just as a child on a basketball team, jumping up and down and waving his arms enthusiastically in the air, anticipates the next event to be his to experience, shouts, "I'm open! I'm open!"—so should we be open . . . to life. And be open . . . to living it.

There are photos in my drawer that when see them, I think, "I wasn't there when I was there." Unfortunately, there are many events that have happened in my life in which my mind was "somewhere else." Though I may have been present physically, I was nowhere in the vicinity mentally. I see now, through the intense clarity of hindsight, that I didn't truly live, soak up, and experience many of these moments, though my body was in attendance. Through remorse, I often feel that, technically, I shouldn't be allowed to even own particular memories, having not fully participated in the occurrences that prompted them. Sometimes I'll feel a pang of guilt claiming I was there because I know in my heart and mind that I really wasn't.

When my youngest daughter was in first grade, her teachers, relatives, and many other adults quickly surmised that she was a fast learner, an extremely detail-oriented child who often remembered little tidbits that might normally be overlooked. They would often tell her that she was very "observant." One day, we walked into a BBQ restaurant we had frequented regularly, and she noted aloud that they had changed the tablecloth colors and the menus. Surprised by her observations, I told her I was impressed that she had remembered such detail. She quickly responded with, "Yes, mommy, that's because I'm very absorbent!" I realized with a smile that she was referring to having been told that she was "observant." Since that day, I have been using this phrase regularly, though I think of it in terms of its intended meaning. I have tried to become, and remain, "absorbent," like a sponge, soaking in details of my surroundings and making mental notes of the unique idiosyncrasies life has to offer. I have been trying to live life in person.

So many of us have somehow become participants in an odd type of competition, one in which life itself is our only opponent. We are overheard saying things like "I just can't keep up" and "I'm so far behind." Not until we realize that as hard as we are able to compete, the trivialities of life will always emerge the victor. They will forever outnumber us, and not until we accept defeat and proudly take second place can we relax and stop running. We start living life in person the day we begin choosing from the list of "could-do" more often than from the list of "should-do." The latter is automatically replenished via a never-ending inventory of details and deadlines; a black hole of tasks that you should do. In direct conflict, the could-do list contains all that is awaiting your arrival, to enjoy and savor. It represents that which you could do, not always after completion of what you should do, but more often instead of what you should do. Truly living life involves finding ways to decrease the length of your should-do, list and increase what you discover and add to your could-do, list. It's been said that we all will die with work undone.

If we live totally, deeply, and in person, we will not face death with apprehension or fear, for we will not feel resentful or embittered, as if we were denied or cheated, at life's conclusion. If we examine every corner of what life has to offer, devoting heart, energy, time, and soul into realizing, appreciating, and relishing this gift, we will be satisfied, filled, and fulfilled, knowing we simply took our turn.

"Live in each season as it passes; breathe the air, drink the drink, taste the fruit, and resign yourself to the influences of each."
—Henry David Thoreau

9-12 PHILOSOPHY

September 11, the most emotional day in the history of my lifetime, left its mental mark upon my mind and soul, as it did on millions of others'. I often write about how everything in this world can teach us a lesson and how there is something invaluable to learn from every occurrence—be it positive or negative. The lessons from that event that were permanently engraved into my heart were not realized on September 11, but on the morning of September 12. After the realization sunk in that this nightmare was indeed a reality, I, with millions of others, felt engulfed in feelings of empathy, appreciation, gratitude, and overwhelming compassion.

As a poet, the only thing I knew that could bring me comfort and allow me to express my grief was to write. I wrote for days as tears fell continuously upon my keyboard. Now, I refer to those writings often. To remind myself to be grateful, I place myself back into that atmosphere mentally, in order to relive my 9-12 Philosophy. In my poem, "My Own Letter to the Terrorists," I wrote:

You've altered thousands of innocent lives, by savagely mangling walls and ceilings . . . but you've unearthed senses in my soul, acquainting me with my own feelings. You've made me want to strive to be, a better person, a kinder being . . . and to replace the fretting and complaining, with more supporting, and agreeing. You've reminded me I have an abundance of love and kindness to extend . . . for there are hopeless who need hope, and friendless to befriend. You've made me eliminate indifference, and the cold effect of nonchalance. Now whenever I ask, "How are you?" I'll stick around for a response. I make these improvements not out of spite, but because I've changed inside . . . and determination has accompanied each and every tear I've cried. If everyone made some loving changes, because of each diverted plane . . . maybe it would help us to believe, that the innocent did not die in vain.

LIFE BUCKS

I would roughly estimate that I am awake and active about 840–960 minutes each day. Yet, I sometimes spend those minutes as if they were seized from an infinite supply, as if a cache of seconds existed somewhere that would continually fill the divots in time left behind by each spent hour. I often spend my allotted minutes haphazardly and without concern or appreciation, with no regard to the reality that minutes are like tea bags, designed for one-time use.

I think of the contrast in what my behavior would be if those minutes were dollars that I was given to spend instead. What if I my life's time was paid to me in life bucks, instead of minutes or hours? I know I would definitely realize the value of what I held in my hands. I would be able to see it, count it, and explore various ways to spend it. I would make sure each time it was relinquished I had gotten the best exchange of value for my dollar. There would be no account to create because I could not bank my bucks, and I might not be granted more tomorrow. I would no doubt spend them with more conscious awareness, more diligence, and more consideration. It is easy to equate spending with money. However, an expenditure can represent an outlay of time as well. Budgeting is simple when you know how much money you'll have, but not when you don't know how many minutes you'll have in your lifetime. That is why the minute you are spending now and in the next rotation of the second hand on the clock should be considered the most valuable of all. Isn't it ironic, that because we can't see, hold, or count them, we often spend our minutes with less regard than we spend our money?

DRIFTING

When we are born and we take in that first deliberate breath on our own, we are signing a binding contract with life. We want to live. Subconsciously, we commit to doing all that we can to experience and relish this remarkable gift that has been bestowed upon us. As toddlers and children, fun, and all that brings us enjoyment, is instinctively our main objective. The exchange of love, smiles, laughter, and affection are that which we seek and yearn for and what makes us complete. We have yet to learn the word *tomorrow*. We have yet to learn enough to shame ourselves into regretting yesterday. What matters is the now. We are not planning, regretting, hoping, and dreaming. We eat what is on our plate and live the life that has been offered to us. We live life in person.

The fact is, as time passes, our youthful mentality slowly erodes as it is replaced with priorities, deadlines, and responsibilities. Slowly, quietly, and unknowingly, the devious waters of success carry us away from living life in person. Yet, it's never too late to begin rowing against these slow-flowing, yet treacherous streams. We are able to shift the currents when we calculate how far we've drifted. We can change direction back to where we began . . . to fulfill the instinctive pledge we made when we breathed in that first breath and signed our contract with life.

When most of us were in grade school, the teacher would recite "roll call" every morning in order to record attendance. We were each expected to respond with an audible "HERE!" to signify our presence when our name was spoken. Over the years, the routine of that daily ritual has remained in my mind. We should all strive to live our lives today so that if life were to take a roll call to determine if we were living in the moment, we would hear our names and instinctively, joyfully respond, "HERE!"

Live Your Dash.

Be HERE

HERE is every moment
that time will allow.
HERE is your life . . .
and it's happening NOW.

HERE is the present
and HERE doesn't last.
It's not linked to your future
nor tied to your past.

HERE cannot be owned;
it is merely to borrow
for what is HERE today
will be gone tomorrow.

HERE is this moment.
HERE is this time.
HERE are the minutes
spent reading this rhyme.

HERE is this instant
in this time and place;
a temporary existence
that we must embrace.

HERE is the show
that will not be rerun.
HERE is soon history
that cannot be undone.

HERE is a sensation.
HERE is a feeling.
HERE are the seconds
time is currently stealing.

Predictably brief
and fleeting is . . . HERE.
It will fade away.
It will disappear.

So live in your now;
be conscious, sincere.
Let your mind allow you
to BE in your HERE.

Don't let past transgressions
and each future plan
deny you the chance
to be HERE while you can!

Density of Life

*D*ensity is defined as "mass multiplied by volume." Thus, the density of life could be defined as the multiplying responsibilities, appointments, schedules, paperwork, deadlines, and commitments that present themselves as both mass and volume in our lives. When we are young, the density of our lives is almost transparent. With our minds clear, our consciences untarnished, and our hearts unbroken, we face the future with unbridled enthusiasm. We can see clearly into the future because we do not yet need to factor density into the equation. As we mature and the demands upon us increase, a dense wall begins to form between living a responsible life and living life itself, creating an obstructed, opaque view. The foundation upon which this wall is built is poured as we begin to make our way through life's journey. Brick by imaginary brick, the wall expands as jobs, relationships, bills, spouses, and children enter our lives, bringing with them added pressures and demands.

However, we don't seem to acknowledge the presence of the wall as it is being formed. Many of us only begin to realize that it is there when its density increases and begins to prevent us from fully experiencing our lives. When mass multiplied by volume begins to surpass pleasure multiplied by joy, we realize we must make changes to stop the pattern. For most, this epiphany occurs somewhere in the middle of middle age. Some are lucky enough to notice it early, by seeing the density begin to thicken in their lives, therefore allowing them to make necessary changes in time. Unfortunately for others, the realization that the density of life has already consumed too much of their vision comes too late.

Life the way we live it can obscure our view of life as it should be lived. We now have "life coaches" inviting us to hire them with advertisements that boast their ability to design a contract that suits both our pocketbook and our goals. I didn't even like my volleyball coach—I don't think I'll be hiring a coach to direct me in how to live my life. Moreover, figuring it out for ourselves, by ourselves, and learning to correct the course of our path when necessary are fundamental parts of the journey. To deny ourselves this introspection would be like focusing so intently on a destination that we miss out on the ride itself.

The density of life causes a cycle of stress that increases in strength as it consumes all that appears in its path. This whirlwind of trivialities can leave irreparable damage in its wake. Every day, we experience an onslaught of material requiring simultaneous brainwave action. Through media—in print, online, on TV, in movies—we are constantly offered incalculable varieties of stimuli that accumulate and add to a density of life that ultimately becomes so thick, it is difficult to shine through. That is why we now have the opportunity to watch "reality shows." Many people feel the only way to shine through the fog of competing stimuli is to behave outlandishly, outrageously, unusually, and unpredictably. They do shocking, often offensive things to help them shine through the dense fog and be noticed. As we read and witness more and more actions committed out of this desperate desire to be noticed, we are slowly becoming desensitized. What my daughters have watched in movies as teenagers without flinching are horrors I could not have envisioned in my worst nightmares when I was their ages. In addition, the more we are deluged with statistics and details, the more we must fight to remain empathetic.

Country singer Loretta Lynn believed in herself and her talents so much that she grabbed her guitar and drove to several radio stations throughout the country to play and sing her songs in person. She and her husband knew that once the folks at the radio station heard and saw her perform, they would give her the break she knew she deserved. Though her confidence and bold tenacity is both admirable and lead to the resounding success she ultimately enjoyed, today you wouldn't be permitted in the studio if you showed up unannounced or unscheduled and requested even a few minutes of airtime. She took a path to success that would be impossible given the density of our atmosphere today. Today, a résumé is often expected to include an associated "network profile." Most publishers won't accept "unsolicited" material from unknown authors, and in this economy, employers can pick and choose from a multitude of workforce candidates. It is increasingly difficult to shine among the stars of the twenty-first century.

Some companies have even deemed it necessary to force consumers to enter into lengthy contracts to begin receiving their services. They, too, have found it increasingly difficult to stand out from the crowd amid the intense and immense competition of the density of life. To provide choices so their services would rise in value above their competitors would mean relinquishing hefty profits. Instead of striving to discover new ways to shine, they have settled for fading into the dark night, satisfied with requiring binding contracts to keep customers, in lieu of offering great customer service, which would likely result in the same outcome.

But, how do you make yourself shine when every day there are more and more brilliant stars appearing seemingly out of oblivion? The best answer is as simple as the lyrics of a song written and recorded in the 1940s: "Ac-Cent-Tchu-Ate the Positive." Rewritten in current jargon, it would translate into: "If you've got it, flaunt it!" It is easy to overlook a single, dull weed in a garden of vibrant blooming flowers, but a single brilliant flower standing proudly in the middle of a bed of weeds draws attention. Seek until you discover ways to become that flourishing flower.

There may be thousands vying for the same position as you, or businesses similar to yours saturating the marketplace, but everyone possesses something unique, something strong, something inherently theirs that can help them to shine. You have within you a talent, skill, or trait that can be enhanced and capitalized upon. Exploit it, even if it takes replacing humility and modesty with confidence and courage.

Social Media

Social media is the name given to various programs for online communication, such as Facebook, MySpace, and Twitter. Although these programs were developed relatively recently, I witnessed examples of an equivalent phenomenon early in my youth. Every summer as a child, my mother and I would spend time in New York City with my grandmother and other relatives. Having been raised in the South, one of the things that fascinated me most was what everyone referred to as "the stoop." The stoop was the concrete set of steps outside each building where residents would (and still do) congregate. You didn't have to call to make an appointment. You didn't have to make reservations. You would just walk outside and secure a spot on one of the steps. Soon you'd be engaged in lively conversation with your neighbors and others who were returning home from work, the local stores, or the park. You could also stop at others' stoops on your way to the deli and visit. It was the equivalent of today's online chat room. It was the first social media. I remember thinking that you would always have friends if you had a stoop. I've often wished since then that the subdivision where I reside had a stoop.

Keyboard Communication

Today's social media and technology, while contributing to the density of life, have created an alarming disconnect in society as well. An unforeseen and unfortunate casualty is person-to-person contact. No longer can local residents of a community talk about the nightly news or articles in the paper, because there are so many options for intellectual input that the odds are against them having seen or read the same information. Whereas they used to share common subjects of conversation from a few popular TV dramas, newscasts, comedies, and entertainment shows, now technology constantly exposes them to thousands of opinions and bits of information daily.

Couples send texts or e-mails to end relationships, children text their parents goodnight from their bedroom upstairs in the same house, a large percentage of relationships are now formed through online communication, and seldom will you find a successful company that doesn't direct customers to their www address. We have even discovered a way to avoid spending time personally shopping for a friend: the gift certificate.

In the computer field, the word *interface* is used to refer to a point of interaction between two components. Basically, it is a conduit that allows hardware and software to communicate. I find use of the term *ironic*, because computers and technology are directly responsible for removing the interface aspect in humans.

FAST TECHNOLOGY

I am not referring to the word *fast* as in quick, speedy, or rapid. I am suggesting we fast from technology more often, as in "to cause to abstain entirely from." It has been said that if we don't manage technology in our lives, it will manage us. I realized the truth in this statement when, in the midst of multitasking recently, I considered, for a nanosecond, sending a text to my dog in the backyard to request that she stop barking.

People fast for religious reasons, in protest, and in preparation for medical tests. Addicts fast from drugs and alcohol to become better people and to become more conscious, more present, in their own lives. Drugs and alcohol have the ability to make a person become someone they don't want to be, often someone they don't even recognize. These substances can change who the person is inside. Technology is slowly changing us too. We are able to use it to escape from our realities and to ignore our responsibilities. Though gambling, drinking, and drugs are a few vices classified as addictives, the use of technology is often justifiably classified as addictive as well.

I won't let an unknown stylist trim my hair, yet I entrust the maintenance of my life to a five-inch combination of metal, plastic, and glass that randomly hoists my personal information over a 4G network. It contains everything my brain cannot remember or has given up trying. It has become an extension of myself. It has become a part of myself. It is my "self phone."

Though I didn't own this wondrous little miracle for the first half of my life, I now experience anxiety symptoms when I am separated from it for any length of time. I sleep with it by my bedside, and it is never more than a few feet from my position. I rely on its accuracy to remember birthdays and anniversaries of friends and relatives and impress my customers daily with rapid response time. Yet, even I, an admitted addict, recognize the need for moderation and occasional abstinence.

I learned about several university students who had participated in a twenty-four-hour fast from technology. They were then requested to blog about their experiences. The words *addiction* and *dependence* appeared often in their compositions. One young woman had commented that even getting into bed was more difficult without the light on her cell phone. Another reported realizing he "had legs" and that they could be used as a social tool to actually go see people in person, rather than communicate wirelessly.

I realize the millions of "Millennials" (a generation whose oldest members are in their thirties and whose youngest are nearing adolescence) exist and thrive in a virtual world in which behaviors such as texting and tweeting are considered the norm. Phrases found most commonly in their vernacular, such as, "Is there an app for that?" and "Did you read his tweet?," still remain foreign to many. The Millennials are technically literate like no generation before them, because technology has always been a part of their lives. The familiar comforts of computers, the Internet, and cell phones have been theirs since many were young children. They view them as vital aspects of their social lives and, as such, necessary and irreplaceable.

With collective identities, generations move on from one decade to the next. If this generation doesn't begin to tap into its human resources once again, these qualities are in danger of being left behind. Increased insensitivity resulting from limited person-to-person contact is the obvious outcome. There is so much value to be found in the human touch and face-to-face communication. Though a technological wonder, a video chat cannot provide a shoulder to catch a tear, a text cannot offer the sympathetic inflection of a kind word, multimedia messages are not able to extend arms to embrace a friend, and an e-mail does not have the capability of holding a hand that needs to be held.

Live Your Dash.

REWIND

Today I closed my eyes and listened
as the waves met the sand on the shore
and slowly a feeling embraced me
as though I'd never heard them before.

I let the world go . . . as I sat by the water;
of every sense, I was fully aware.
I felt the breeze from the ocean as it entered my lungs
and randomly blew through my hair.

In my mind, I erased the duties and tasks
through my days, I'm expected to do
for I'm finally realizing this about life:
such moments are fleeting and few.

But . . . what if technology were so advanced,
we could use it to move through life . . .
to fast forward through the sadness
and scroll over struggles and strife?

We could pause all the wonderful moments
and hit play, again and again
and wear out the rewind button
going back to wherever we'd been.

The restore key could bring back loved ones
or repair a wilted flower
and we could use the insert button
to put more minutes in each hour!

185

We could backspace over our mistakes,
save each memory as a file,
click delete for each and every tear
and screen capture every smile.

But life has no rewind button
and we cannot save each day;
there is no pause to stop the time
from slowly fading away.

So, until there's a key on my keyboard
that reads: repeat this day once more . . .
I'll slow down and live my life "in the now"
like I've never . . . ever . . . lived it . . . before.

Failure to Affix

The density of life causes side effects and leaves collateral damage in its path. Not until a close relative swallowed a suppository before a colon exam, assuming it was a pill, did I truly believe that fundamental warnings and specific instructions that seem so obvious were necessary. When something is purchased in a box and the contents are wrapped in a plastic bag, the package usually contains a bold printed warning NOT to place the bag over a child's head. One would think such a warning would not be necessary, but with the diversions and interruptions of today, coupled with our litigious society, such warnings are essential. Because of the density of life, and the fatal distractions technology has created, we need to be consistently reminded of basic information. We need all the help we can get.

When I was seventeen years old, I was pulled over for speeding by a southern state trooper whose outward appearance did not vary much from the law officers portrayed in movies who wear widely brimmed Smokey the Bear hats and vow to sternly uphold the law. Fully believing at that time I was far cuter than I actually appeared to that officer, I tried to talk my way out of a ticket. However, I soon drove away with a very expensive traffic violation, and an ego-bursting life lesson. That was the only traffic ticket I'd ever received, so naturally, twenty years later, the unfamiliar blue lights flickering in my rear view mirror startled me. Instantly, my mind raced back to replay any possible infraction I may have committed at that last intersection. Full stop . . . turn signal . . . green light . . . all seemed well. Why then, was the patrol car behind my vehicle motioning me to pull over?

I found a safe area to stop and a policeman resembling Mayberry's Barney Fife slowly approached my car. The look on his face made me instantly feel like a Bonnie without a Clyde. Had my infraction been severe enough to warrant such a harsh expression? I asked as politely and innocently as I believed I truly was, "What's wrong, officer?" He replied, "Afternoon ma'am. You don't have a current registration sticker on your license plate. This year's sticker is green, and yours is still orange." "That's impossible!" I retorted. Instantly regretting my statement's vehemence and unintended tone, I added, "Office . . . Sir . . ."

"I have it right here," I stated as I frantically searched the glove compartment for the registration. An old Willie Nelson CD . . . a pack of gum . . . a tube of lipstick, and aha! I found it! I clearly recognized the document and opened it up eagerly to defiantly display it for him and wait patiently for his apology. As I handed it to him, however, a little green sticker glared at me from the top corner of the document, as if it was mocking me. The words "Barney is right" were almost audible.

I couldn't believe it. I distinctly recalled visiting the tag office months before. I remembered because the kids were fighting when we'd returned to the car, it had started to thunder and I was rushing home because I had forgotten to feed the dogs that hectic morning. I could remember every detail, except removing the sticker from the registration and placing it on to my license plate.

Well, no problem. I'm sure Mr. Fife here will understand when I explain it to him. Assuming he probably wasn't interested in the hungry dog portion of my excuse, I went straight to the fix it segment of my story, stating, "Well, thank you so much for bringing this to my attention. I'll just put that little sucker on my plate right now. Have a wonderful evening, officer . . . and I'll be sure to send my donation to the Police Benevolence Association again this year . . ."

I couldn't believe what I heard next: "Ma'am, I'm issuing you a citation." "A citation?" I exclaimed. "For what?" "For failure to display your current registration sticker on your license plate. It's the law here in the state of Georgia," he answered without emotion, as if he was reading the fifth paragraph from the rookie officer handbook. "You can't be serious," I said. "I just forgot to put it on. It was right here in my vehicle!" With an undeniable note of sarcasm, coupled with a cat-that-ate-the-canary grin, he responded, "Now how was I supposed to see that from my patrol car?" He had me there. I shook my head in disbelief and asked, "How much will the ticket be?" "Well, if you go to court and show them that you had a valid registration, the judge may go easy on you," he answered. I felt, the way conversation was headed, it was in my best interest not to repeat what I was thinking, which was, "Is it just me, or does this scenario seem a little bit silly to you?"

I bit my tongue and left with the yellow copy of my admonishment, which stated I was to appear in court on the sixteenth of the month. In my mind, I was already planning to be the first one let in the courtroom that day, registration in hand. This would mean missing some time from work and rearranging my schedule, but the law is the law, and I was out to set a good example for my children.

On the morning of the sixteenth, I drove directly to the courthouse, as planned, in high hopes of returning to the office for a late-morning meeting. I sat down with the proper posture of a Catholic schoolgirl and folded my hands neatly on my lap. Wearing what I deemed my judge-impressing navy-blue suit and white blouse, I'm sure I appeared more like a courteous flight attendant than a scofflaw.

As I had anticipated, I was the first one allowed into the room by the burly courthouse bouncers. I carefully selected a seat in the front pew, foolishly believing that the early bird gets the worm. The bailiff began to read names aloud, one after the other. I tried to detect in what order my fellow lawbreakers were being lead to the pulpit and where my name might fall on their list of Violators and Infractors list. Alphabetically? No, because Mr. Martin just went before Ms. Kern. I soon understood that the V&I list was apparently arranged sequentially by date of infraction. I assumed that I must live in a first-come, first-serve county. As the hours slowly passed, I tried to ease my anxiety by keeping my mind busy with random thoughts. I found myself wondering from what wood the judge's podium was made and how many bathroom breaks he was allotted in one day. I peered out the window at a curious squirrel staring back at me and wondered if these proceedings were nothing more than a show on Court TV for him.

When I had just completed my comparison of the total number of ceiling tiles on the left side of the room versus the right, the woman next to me began to chat. I wasn't eager to make a new best friend, but I'm always open to a good conversation. I turned toward her and briefly wondered, while trying desperately not to be judgmental, how her bodily fluids remained contained within the sieve that was now her body. Her piercings began through her eyebrows and continued to points beyond. She began describing each of her tattoos, the knife blade on her left arm and the tiger shark on her right. "That one reminds me of my mother," she stated proudly. "You have her eyes," I responded compassionately.

As if by silent invitation, her friend joined in our newly formed support group and they began comparing details about the evenings that apparently ensured their presence in Judge Ramey's courtroom that morning. They seemed to take pride describing the bravado they'd displayed while they were handcuffed in front of a crowd. I found myself so shaken and shocked by the details of Stella's admission of drug sales and possession and Brandy's weapons charges, I must admit, I inconspicuously shifted about four inches toward the left side of the bench. I was attempting, unsuccessfully, to avoid "the question" I knew would certainly be coming my way.

And then, it came. "So, why are YOU here?" they both asked. As is suggested when one is the victim of a grizzly bear attack, I remained still and pretended not to hear the question over the relative silence of the courtroom. Stella asked again, louder, assuming my nonresponse must be due to a terrible hearing impairment. I turned my head and acted as though I'd been interrupted midstream during a cough, passing my right hand over my lips as I answered humbly with something that sounded vaguely like "Falla tala fistaroo . . ." "What?" they both repeated in unison. "Falura to aviksitate . . ." I mumbled. I was hoping the inquisitiveness of Thelma and Louise would come to an end soon, but no luck. "Huh?" they repeated. It was obvious to me that I wasn't going to escape the inquisition. Adopting a "when in Rome" philosophy, I snapped, "FAILURE TO AFFIX!" I almost felt some level of disappointment that my crime had little chance at making any impression on them. (Had I actually been, caught up in the moment, seeking their respect and admiration for my misdeed?) They both smirked disapprovingly, and I realized I had to resign myself to the fact that I probably wouldn't be receiving an invitation to join their sorority. My life of crime thwarted, I felt the bench shift as they both moved inconspicuously a few inches to the right.

When it was my turn to see the judge, I walked slowly to the front of the courtroom with my head down, like a dog with his tail between his legs. Having never faced a judge, I stood with enough external remorse to make any outsider looking in believe I had committed a heinous crime. I noticed the squirrels had now gathered outside the window, and I began explaining my situation in earnest. Though I tried to be succinct in my account, my nerves got the better of me, and I rattled on about the kids fighting, the storm, and the unfed dogs from the evening in question. Then I held my vehicle registration up in front of the judge like a proud kindergartner who had finished a new finger painting. The judge reviewed my paperwork, glanced down at my apologetic expression, and, I believe, took pity on me after he learned of my transgressions. I was a free woman.

As I left the courtroom, I turned and bid farewell to my newfound friends and wished them both well. They shunned me and looked away, and I thought about how fickle they had become in just a short while. I drove home thinking how it is these details in life—the small yet necessary responsibilities that fill every day—that accumulate and often replace what should take priority. This task would've taken less than sixty seconds to complete had it not represented one in a hundred that day, and ultimately cost me dearly because I paid a fine with my most valued and irreplaceable asset: my time.

ON
MOMENTS

Fractions

Give 100 percent of yourself to everything you do. This is great advice, but in today's multitasking world, the idea is virtually impossible. Furthermore, when and if you do manage to accomplish this feat, something, somewhere must suffer the consequences. You're an employee, a colleague, a boss, a parent, a spouse, a friend, a sibling, a daughter, or a son. Yet, you are not these things singularly, you are all of these things and more, simultaneously. Out of desperation and necessity, you attempt to divide yourself, in fractions, accordingly. You devote a percentage of yourself and time to be a parent, to be an employee, to be a spouse, to be a friend. However, when you are through doing the math, what percentage is left to just be you?

Though you may not be able to literally devote 100 percent of yourself to something or someone, you can ensure that the percentage of attention you are able to provide is, at least temporarily, undivided. Multitasking is an art, a talent honed through living and thriving through the density of life today. It is the skill of being able to efficiently and competently perform several tasks simultaneously. It is the ability to master instantly dividing your attention and focus, into fractions. Rather than focusing on one task and then another, it requires the spanning of the same amount of attention across a multitude of undertakings.

While performing this skill, it is not required to devote to each task, undivided attention. In fact, capitalizing on dispersing undivided attention is the core talent and perfected ability of an efficient multitasker. The unfortunate side effect is that we continue to multitask when that which is happening around us does not qualify as "tasks." Multitasking becomes a habit that silently infuses itself into our daily routines. The result is that we multi-walk, we multi-talk, we multi-experience, we multi-live, we multi-moment. For the sake of simplification, let's fraction the whole being into four main components: body, mind, heart, and soul. These parts are all naturally, inextricably connected. You cannot give 100 percent of one without tapping into another. Most of us appear to have a larger percentage of some components than others, but we comprise basically an equal amount of each. Tasks as defined in this article are classified as everyday jobs, errands, duties, responsibilities. They require, for the most part, the mind and body. Moments, on the contrary, are more likely to use the heart and the soul.

Very few things in life keep our attention long enough to experience and absorb them. Many of us find it a necessity to multitask, but it is vital to our well-being that we give ourselves fully to the moments. To do so, we need to focus on the important distinctions between a task and a moment. Tasks will always be present; moments are transient. Unaccomplished tasks can be moved to a later date; moments cannot be postponed. Tasks are scheduled; moments, often spontaneous. Tasks are prevalent; moments, elusive. Most importantly, the incompletion of a task cannot compare to the lifelong regret of missing a special moment.

I'VE LEARNED TO DIFFERENTIATE

EACH MOMENT FROM EACH MINUTE:

A MINUTE IS BUT A MEASURE OF TIME,

BUT A MOMENT IS WHAT'S IN IT.

Live Your Dash.

MOMENTS

Our lives are measured by the minutes
which turn the hours into years,
but remembered by the moments
made of laughter, love and tears.

It is life's moments that define the years
and chronicle our past . . .
mile markers of a journey
that is over much too fast.

Those moments that may leave behind
a secret smile or a scar
are the notable, quotable happenings
that make us who we are.

It is the moments that we capture
while in our minds we create
indelible pictures of the time we spend
as precious seconds dissipate.

Routine hours may fill our days
as simple blocks of time . . . until
a moment makes it seem as though
the world is standing still.

Today's moments are not forever;
only a while do they last.
And we all are living legacies
of moments that have passed.

In our memories, the years will blur;
dates and times will fall apart,
but moments are like epitaphs
engraved upon a heart.

Life's moments . . . precious gifts;
more treasured than silver or gold...
invaluable, intangible,
and precious to behold.

New moments lie ahead each day;
they are there as we awaken.
We should ask ourselves when the day is done,
"Were there moments left untaken?"

Spontaneous or well-rehearsed,
causing laughter . . . causing pain.
They may happen in the sunshine;
they may happen in the rain.

But moments turn into memories,
what you've done . . . where you've been,
and in each memory, each moment
can be lived and lived again.

Fleeting minutes of time may pass,
to be recalled maybe never.
Let us savor in life . . . the moments
for they will stay with us forever.

Savor the Flavor . . . of Life

I was busy cleaning my kitchen when some unusual movement caught my eye through the glass doors. I walked over to glance into the backyard. Suddenly, a gust of wind seemingly originating from every direction intensified so that it set free every brown, yellow, and orange leaf from the grip the old oak had on them during the months of spring and summer. I stood motionless as they cascaded down, twirling and swirling in different directions as though they had been rehearsing a synchronized dance routine together. In one fell swoop, the brisk breeze had created a virtual snowfall of autumn leaves, and I was admittedly mesmerized by the scene. I imagined myself standing underneath that tree, arms extended, head up, and eyes closed. I could almost feel the gentle brush of the leaves as my skin interrupted their graceful journey downward. I wanted to walk beneath the tree and hear the crunching sound of those fallen leaves underneath my footsteps.

I was pleased with myself for pausing my hasty cleaning to witness this spontaneous event—an event I would normally not have noticed. Yet on this day, I felt as if I had been the sole attendee of a brief, yet breathtaking, exhibition being performed by Mother Nature herself in a scene no downloadable app could ever reenact.

I thought how wonderful it would be to videotape a short bit of the experience in order to watch it again and hopefully recreate the awe I'd felt when it occurred. I ran upstairs to grab the camera and returned to the scene in hopes of capturing nature's encore. I walked outside on the deck and stood still in the cool air and waited with my camera in the palm of my hand, aiming toward the leaves that remained at the top of the tree. Through the camera's viewfinder, I focused on their warm, muted hues as I mentally decided which angle and zoom to use to follow the spiralling, uncharted route of their voyage to their new destination. Their fate now was only to play an essential role in the next phase of the circle of life.

I waited patiently. Then, I waited impatiently. I waited . . . and waited. However, I soon realized that the uncooperative wind had ceased to move entirely. Though the smell of the crisp, fall air had me feeling tranquil and serene, I was nonetheless disappointed when it occurred to me I had missed the opportunity to capture "my" moment on film. The continued silence only served to convince me that I had been given the chance to seize this unique experience only in my mind, as a vivid memory. It was as though at that moment, I'd imagined choosing "save file" on the keyboard of my computer so that I might relive this inspiration by later extracting it from the database of memories and moments we all keep in the archives of our minds.

It was obvious to me that my options were indeed limited: I could learn to savor the flavor of life, which is doled out in increments known as "moments," or live with my Nikon strapped around my neck 24/7. I have chosen to savor . . . how about you?

Embrace the moments. Commit to living your life in the moment more often. Whatever you are involved in, embrace it fully. Learn to occupy each moment and reside in the now. By trying to take on everything going on in your life at once, you are missing out on the moments that truly make up your life. It is the "moments" that you will cherish and remember.

Senses

Senses: The physiological capacities within organisms that provide inputs for perception. Although I contend that they are SO much more than that . . .

Have you ever caught the brief aroma of a familiar blooming flower or saw a passing, recognizable image from the corner of your eye or heard an old song on the radio and literally been taken back in your mind to a different place and time in your life?

Though sight, hearing, touch, smell, and taste may be our five fundamental "inputs for perception," I've discovered that each also has a unique attribute and capability that is often overlooked. It connects. Each is a channel through which a current experience, within seconds, is matched to even the most minute details of a corresponding memory. These details, from a practicality standpoint, should have vanished forever just like the hours in the days in which they occurred. However, they have been strategically filed away instead, deep into our memories only to be brought forth by a common bond, unearthed and subsequently "matched" by one or more of our senses to a current happening. Seeing, hearing, touching, smelling, and tasting all have the ability to effortlessly, seamlessly unite our present to our past and repeat this scenario with every occurrence of a particular experience.

For me, one perfect example of this theory from many is the sweet, pungent, yet pleasing fragrance of blooming gardenias. When I was a child, our next-door neighbor had a huge gardenia bush, which seemed to be perpetually in bloom. (The shrub was so large and boasted such sharp, prickly leaves that the recollection of it today brings to mind an image of Seymour's "plant" in *Little Shop of Horrors* shouting, "Feed Me"!) I had often visited that neighbor's house during my childhood. Today, whenever our gardenia bush is in bloom and I catch that unique scent as I pass it by in haste, I instantly become that little girl standing on my neighbor's front porch. It's as though I'm obliged by my mind to escape back in time. I feel compelled to pause the constant forward motion of my life and reflect on details I thought were long forgotten.

Another scenario I've witnessed again and again involves lyrics and songs. There are countless songs you've enjoyed, sung aloud, and replayed over and over but may not have heard in many years. Suddenly, you're driving along and a particular song plays on the radio. Before you realize what's happening, you are singing every word, every tone variance, every note in tune with the songster. Where has all this information been all this time? The sense of hearing—the conduit—matched, opened, and poured out the contents of that song's file from your mind. You associate it with friends who sang along, places you'd heard it performed or swaying to its rhythm with a young lover as hazy images begin to flood your brain and you relive that moment in time.

Imagine a roadmap displaying many roads leading from the town square, each route, a never-ending path leading out into the world, yet originating from the same core destination. These roads represent our senses and the town square holds our memories. Each road has its own direct route back to the town square and individually connects us at will, as we continue life's journey.

Many find comfort and solace in the virtual photos and unique memories captured and sporadically brought forth by our senses. I smile whenever I watch the tropical birds at the ocean and without fail, when I see a lone pelican standing proudly on a piece of driftwood, I can clearly hear my dad's voice bellow: "The strange bird is a pelican . . . his beak can hold more than his belly can."

For many it's the sweet aroma of baking cookies that takes them instantly back to grandma's house or the sound of crashing waves that mentally transports them to collecting seashells with siblings on a memorable summer vacation. Billowing clouds passing overhead will, for some, conjure visions of lying on a cool field of grass with a special childhood friend, uncovering hidden images in the cloud's formations; and the taste of a fresh strawberry on someone's tongue can bring from the past a fruitful backyard garden.

Senses and memories are irreversibly intertwined, forever. Relive your life's moments by allowing your senses to carry you back to favorite times and places. Slow down enough to appreciate and absorb the nuances of the cherished memories your senses carry with them.

Scars and Memories

Anybody moves, she gets it . . ." Twenty-five years later, those words ring in my ears as though I'd heard them yesterday. They were spoken by an unknown entity standing in front of me, whose raspy voice I didn't recognize and whose face remains in my mind as nothing more than a masked silhouette in a poorly lit hallway. Yet that voice, that silhouette, and that day left behind a scar in my psyche that time has yet to heal.

As he firmly motioned us to the room in back of the building, I remember feeling his sinister presence walking behind me. I can still feel that uneasy curiosity parading through my mind that day as he followed us, walking slowly and deliberately into the storeroom. It was a morbid curiosity of what the bullet he would surely be sending in my direction might feel like as it penetrated my skin. To this day, that memory brings with it an eerily haunting sensation, along with the inescapable thoughts of a "what if" scenario.

After he had herded seven of us like cattle into the storeroom, I never turned my head to look back. I faced the wall, standing still, adjacent to a concrete pillar that, at the time, provided support for both the building and my body. I squeezed my hands together until my fingers turned white from lack of free-flowing blood. I began to pray. I prayed so hard, if felt as though my brain began to hurt. I squinted my eyes as if that might somehow expedite my desperate pleas on their journey upward. I focused and prayed so honestly, I made up for every minute of every Sunday I'd ever missed in church.

The gun he had held was like the delete button on a keyboard. Gone in an instant was a part of the innocence I'd possessed through my childhood and into my young adult years. For the first time, death became more of a realization than a visualization to me, and suddenly, as a very strong possibility. The thief took with him much more than money as he fled the scene that evening, because he had also stolen pieces of my spirit's purity, hope, and optimism. It was the single most pivotal turning point in the carefree attitude of an untarnished soul.

In my mind, I can still take myself back to the feeling of leaning against that stone-cold pillar. I jokingly comment today that I might still be there with my hands folded if not for the mass exodus of my fellow victims through a window that opened into the dark alley. I remember the cold night air filling my lungs as I ran the fastest I'd ever run toward safety.

That unfortunate incident from my youth left scars, though not visible, more prevalent than those that may have resulted had I survived a bullet that day. Proving that although most of our noticeable scars are linked to memories, memories can, in turn, leave permanent scars. Perhaps that one-inch enduring blemish on your left hand resulted from a mishap with a box cutter when you were thirteen, and that three-inch disfigurement on your abdomen from emergency removal of an internal organ many years ago. With the aid of necessary medical care, and often without, our body is pre-programmed to heal our external wounds, resulting usually in scars that carry with them only memories of the pain.

However, the wounds that occur below the surface are often deeper and slower to heal. It is these invisible scars we bear that do not have the advantage of being protected, medicated, and nursed back to health. There are no emotional bandages with salve we can apply, no stitches to repair invisible gashes. Internal wounds have free range to fester, and they will spread like an untreated cancer will metastasize. Time may heal all wounds, but the scars may still remain forever.

AFTER WORDS

Words are one of the greatest gifts and one of the most lethal weapons we have at our disposal at all times. If words were physical objects, their value could be equated to liquid gold and their ability to slice to that of the sharpest blade of any knife. How misleading the children's chant, "Sticks and stones may break my bones, but words can never hurt me," for words spoken in anger have the capability to cause invisible cuts that never stop bleeding. Even when we are the donor and not the recipient, the repercussions or regret from using certain words at certain times toward or against others, that which happens after words, can haunt us forever.

"Sorry seems to be the hardest word." A catchy cliché, but technically, incomplete. Expressing a sincere apology may not be easy, but simply saying "I'm sorry" and expecting immediate absolution is not realistic. Though the two words may have the ability to ease tension and minimize pain, they cannot alone expunge the past by eliminating that which has been spoken and that which has been heard. Moreover, there are many who use the phrase to their advantage and are always prepared to repeat it after words. The true meaning and intent of the phrase, to them, has been lost due to its overuse. Their readiness to apologize after words gives them a green light, subconsciously, to proceed with speaking harmful, hurtful words.

Many of us as kids used the term *do over*. When a ball was kicked or batted out of bounds, but the two sides reached an impasse on the details of the event, someone would shout, "Do over!" and the play could resume as if the ball's journey beyond the boundary line had never transpired. However, in life and love, there are no do overs. We cannot speak hateful expressions in the heat of the moment or with revenge as our intent and later apologize because permanent damage is done as soon as the utterance is complete. Sometimes the hurt we cause is immediately evident and satisfying if that was the intent, and often the words can linger, reviving the victim's pain repeatedly for years.

HURTFUL WORDS AND MEMORIES

AFFECT WHO AND WHAT WE ARE . . .

THOUGH WE MAY NEVER SEE

THE WOUNDS THEY CAUSE,

WE'LL ALWAYS BEAR THE SCAR.

Equally as powerful as words spoken negatively are those that have positive results as well. Heartfelt words of praise, recognition, and support have the ability to turn around a day, an attitude, a life. Just as words of negativity can create lasting pain, the pleasure and good memories positive words generate can also remain forever. We must not, however, confuse empty greetings with heartfelt praise and appreciation. Spewing insincere compliments as conversation icebreakers or greetings may cause a brief, positive reaction in a returned nod or smile, but insincerity can shine through like a beacon in the night. It is the genuine words of admiration, congratulations, and support that have the ability to create a wonderful mutually positive effect, both on the receiver and the giver.

RECOGNITION

Words of recognition provide perhaps the most simple, yet priceless after words effect. Everyone appreciates being appreciated. People take pleasure in an acknowledgment of their invested efforts, whether they admit to it or not. The slightest show of gratitude has the potential to touch a heart far beyond what may be outwardly expressed. Sharing the two syllables of the two words *Thank You* or *Good Job*, expressed genuinely, often creates everlasting results.

My husband and I learned early the powerful effect of these phrases. When we were potty training our first child, we would repeatedly say, "Good Girl!" when she would do as instructed. The praise and recognition we bestowed accordingly and the strategy of commending each accomplishment quickly proved to be an effective method that reaffirmed our confidence as young parents. One particular morning, as the tot-in-training was walking past the bathroom, she suddenly stopped and stood motionless in the hallway, after hearing the toilet flush. I watched curiously as she stood silently outside the bathroom. When the door soon opened and her father exited, she immediately, enthusiastically began clapping her hands while exclaiming: "Good Girl, Daddy!"

Contributors

Everyone you've met, or will meet, or haven't met but know of, is a contributor. Every friend, foe, co-worker, family member, or casual acquaintance represents a single thread that is woven through the fabric of your life. Some contributors remain in your life forever, some for a week, some for a random summer. However, they each impart one or more contributions to your life, and these gifts are the input that eventually encompasses your memories, shapes your opinions and views, and teaches you invaluable lessons. Contributors are like a coalition of sculptors molding our lives as our journey continues.

Right place, right time. All the people, all the experiences, be they positive or negative, happen at the right time and placement in your lifespan . . . because you are a product of them. Without everything that has happened to you, the good and the bad, you would not be the person who you are. Through life everyone eventually serves as both a teacher and a student. As recipients of contributions, we need to remain cognizant that we are contributors for others, as well.

I reflect often on what has been instilled in my mind through the many contributors to my dash. A past boss, Al Finch, taught me that "almost" everything is negotiable. My mother's greatest verbal contribution was her belief and repetition of the statement, "Things are only material and can be replaced." My brother Bill contributed how important it is to keep smiling . . . no matter how bad things get . . . and to sing aloud if it makes you happy. (No matter how annoying it is to others.) My dad contributed by example how to live, and die, with dignity. My brother Jim through the life he lives contributed that God is good, and my brother John contributed the importance of maintaining the ability to persevere.

However, contributions are not solely provided by people. They can be felt and experienced via animals, nature, and other avenues of life. The smell of a rose, the sight of a sunset, the purr of a kitten, a loving nuzzle from a puppy, the sweet taste of a fresh and ripened peach—all add and contribute to our lives in their own ways.

Think about the contributors in your life, even those you remember with less than fond recollection. Focus on the contributions they each left with you, both the positive and the negative. Connect their contributions with aspects of your life: experiences, decisions, outcomes, paths, opinions. Think about that which you have contributed and continue to contribute to others. Realize the effect your actions have had, and will have, on those who receive your contributions.

YOUR LIFE IS A CONTINUOUS PORTRAIT,

PAINTED MORE COLORFUL EVERY DAY

FROM THE BRUSH STROKES OF THE PEOPLE

YOU MEET ALONG THE WAY.

ON
TIME

Invitations

We all receive invitations as the years roll on, requesting our presence at various events and functions. Most will ask for a timely response so that our host can plan the event accordingly. Basically, we have the option of checking yes to indicate that we plan to mark it on our calendar or no if we have a previously scheduled commitment or simply have chosen not to participate for one reason or another.

Lately however, I've been approaching this from a different point of view. I've begun to focus on a concept I refer to as "Life Invitations." I've suddenly realized that my life has been continually sending to me personal, VIP invitations to experience the joys, the beauties, and the endless wonders it has to offer. Before this new viewpoint, I had left many of those invitations unanswered and many times, hadn't even recognized their presence. Now I see them everywhere and after truly realizing the brevity of some and the significance of others, I feel compelled to respond positively in most instances.

If the invitations life sends to us were tangible, they'd arrive with parchment paper inside shimmering foil envelopes, embossed with only the option to "Accept" written in letters of gold. Every morning as we awaken, during every hour of every day with which we are blessed and with every setting sun, these "invitations" are patiently awaiting our RSVP. We may not receive them in our mailbox or in an e-mail, but they are life's parties, and we are cordially invited to attend.

They are subtle, yet blatantly obvious when recognized, as they silently beckon us to explore, discover, experience and feel life itself. However, the busier our lives become and the more responsibilities and deadlines we place upon ourselves and our schedules, the less time we have available to allow us to check that "Accept" box.

A blooming rose sends an invitation to every passerby to stop and enjoy the aroma of its petals. A gentle rainfall on a summer day sends an invitation to experience the cool drops of water falling upon our shoulders. The autumn leaves send an invitation to drink in their wondrous hues and witness the graceful ballet of their inevitable descent from the trees. Each sunset and sunrise sends an invitation to observe in awe its magnificence as one descends beyond the horizon signifying the conclusion of a day and the latter arrives with the promise of another. The sound of a child's laughter can warm the coldest heart if we pause long enough to pay attention . . . not to hear, but to listen.

There is a difference between skimming the surface of life and truly experiencing it, and it is profound. It is the difference between hearing . . . and listening, between touching and feeling, between eating and tasting, between floating where the current takes you and rowing toward a destination.

When non-participation is your immediate response to a Life Invitation, ask yourself honestly: Why? What are the reasons why you cannot dive into what brings you joy? Is it because of time constraints? Is it because your task list contains too many inconsequential commitments? Is it time to reprioritize your to-do list by using the "delete" key? Is it time to start answering excessive requests of your time with the word, no"?

As we grow older and the time in between years seems to magically accelerate, we realize how very important it is to begin responding positively more often to these special invites. Life's blessings are infinite and we need to take them in . . . one by one. The invitations we've ignored and the times we've chosen not to participate begin to weigh more heavily upon our shoulders, resulting in regret. We begin to realize the longer we're here, the less time remains, and it becomes more important than ever to take advantage of every opportunity to dive into life's waters.

There is a humorous comparison of life to a roll of toilet paper, because it goes faster the closer you get to the end. Everyone, as they grow older, will at some point agree that this concept begins to feel more like a fact than a joke.

Live Your Dash.

TOMORROW'S YESTERDAY

We rue the passing of each yesterday
because it is, forever gone
and take for granted that we'll live to see
another break of dawn.

Time eagerly moves forward;
though we may plead, it never lingers.
Intangible yet, we feel its presence
as it slips right through our fingers.

It progresses callously onward
like an illness with no cure,
while we anticipate tomorrow
as if it was ours, for sure.

Precious seconds tick in rhythm
as we walk . . . and laugh . . . and sleep,
accumulating into minutes
that we can use, but never keep.

Today is here, but only once,
a blessing . . . merely ours to borrow,
for it will soon turn into yesterday . . .
just as it was once, tomorrow.

Minutes to hours, hours to days,
no secret or mystery . . .
our "now" in turn, becomes our "then"
. . . a part of our life's history.

Live for today . . . live for your "now,"
make memories that will last;
paint bold colors of your present
to the canvas of your past.

Don't postpone your hopes and dreams
by saying . . . "I'll be happy when . . . "
Seize the seconds that are passing by
for you can't get them back again!

Learn to savor these 24 hours
without one minute of delay,
because too soon they will forever be . . .
tomorrow's yesterday.

AAA (Age, Awareness, Appreciation)

A ge, awareness, and appreciation. They are bestowed upon our lives in that order and one of them cannot be fully functional, even after it is attained, without having the added value of experiencing its predecessor.

Age: something we do not achieve, nor choose; something most of us do not anticipate with eagerness; something, despite our unsuccessful attempts to ignore, is consistently present in our daily lives; and something we, for the most part, devote our time and money battling. Age is the constant that our lives evolve around. With age comes an attachment—maturity—which arrives at different degrees, at different stages, for different people. Some seem to possess maturity beyond their years and others, whether by choice or fate, never achieve the level of maturity that is equal to the number of years their lives have tallied.

Awareness: cannot be achieved without having lived long enough to compare one experience to another. It is a subliminal byproduct occurring during the aging and maturing process. Each occurrence of awareness is an unexpected realization derived from a brand new insight. The process of experiencing various forms of awareness is a fundamental, integral, and imperative step one must experience before any life improvement strategy can be implemented. Awareness is a subconscious effort, happening naturally, involuntarily, when one suddenly absorbs the truth and, thereby, ceases to distort reality.

Appreciation: cannot be fully realized without having had the epiphanies, aha! moments, conscious alerts, and sudden instances of clarity that go off in our minds like firecrackers as we become more aware of how the individual "pieces" begin to fit into our life's puzzle. As our journey progresses, so does the awareness of that which life generously grants us, which ultimately results in our gratitude, hence, our appreciation.

I do not believe that youth, by lacking age, also lacks awareness and appreciation; however, the latter of the three certainly becomes far more apparent as we experience, and become aware of, the value in our various life lessons.

These three A's occur and advance every day we are alive, always in the same order. Simply put, the more we age, the more we become aware of all that we have to appreciate.

I read two quotes whose contradiction continues to intrigue me:

"Right now, you are the youngest you will ever be."

"Right now, you are the oldest you have ever been."

How is it feasible that we can be both at the same time? This is one of the mysteries of living and of life. Think about these two perceptions in reference to how you honestly view the remaining time in your own dash. If you had to choose one, based on how you feel about your life today, which one would it be, to consider yourself more the youngest you will ever be or the oldest you have ever been? Which view would you prefer be applicable to your life? What viewpoints and perspectives would you have to reverse in your mind to make your preference a reality? What is stopping you?

TIME THIEVES

Though we allow them to expend precious minutes of our time, their actions still constitute theft by taking! Not only do they greedily appropriate portions of our current lives, many of these scoundrels continue to rob us year after year. They will continue their piracy as long as we permit them to do so. These burglars have the capability to hijack our present minutes of contentment and joy. Somehow they manage to immediately replace them with angry, stressful minutes instead. Individually they are invisible, weightless, yet they are incredibly powerful. Combined, they can be toxic. Though they possess the element of surprise, we are not defenseless to stop them. The secret is to stifle their existence at first sight of their arrival, for the longer they are free to roam, the larger and more influential they become and the more precious time they will steal.

Remorse and regret, like haunting apparitions, have the capability to constantly hover over your days and nights. They will never be exorcised until they are released. They are the time thieves that grab hold of your conscience and refuse to release their grip. Directly responsible for tears shed and sleepless nights, they slyly appear when we least expect them and before we are fully aware, we have relinquished even more of our "now" to their gluttonous grasp. Forgiveness and mercy are their enemies. The repeated practice of granting pure and unconditional absolution in our hearts will eventually pull in the reins that control their power over us.

Worry is the worst type of time thief because it represents minutes spent in anguish over that which may or may never happen. It's as though we have written a blank check payable to Angst that is cashed over and over again. I've often read that worrying is like paying interest on a loan before it ever becomes due. Don't let tomorrow's hypothetical problems subtract from today's definite joy!

Frustration is the most compliant time thief because it can be frequently anticipated and most often expected. We know what frustrates us, and yet we allow our reactions to perpetuate the thievery. Frustration is just a culmination of annoyances, nuisances, and aggravations. Tolerance, acceptance, and patience are frustration's foes. Utilizing all three will eliminate frustration and reclaim its theft of our time.

Hatred is the vilest bandit of all time thieves. We, its victims, suffer losses greater than time. Completely devoid of rational thought or compassion, it possesses the power to steal our minutes through a hostile takeover of our senses. Of course to combat hatred, we need to envelop it in love until it dissolves like sugar. Only when we truly realize its destructive potential, are we able to recognize and slay its invasive claw as soon as it punctures our peace. The root of evil is the time thief of hatred. When you allow this villain inside, it will steal joyful minutes from you, your friends, and your loved ones and burn them like fuel.

Anger is perhaps the most useless, unproductive time thief. Like the others, it leaves nothing positive or valuable behind. It serves no purpose except to provide a medium for the eventual emergence of its cousins: regret and remorse. Like a hungry lion, it can spring from out of nowhere and attack with a vengeance. Often it hides in the shadows, waiting for opportunities or unfortunate antagonists to rear their ugly heads. Left unattended, it has the potential to permeate every aspect of our lives. How much damage it inflicts is solely dependent on how many times you let it circle the drain before allowing it to disappear forever. Understanding is anger's nemesis, consideration its foe.

Discontent, continuously walking in the shadows of the road not taken, is a major time thief. Its effect is mentally exhausting, and it prevents us from experiencing gratitude and peace. Minutes spent in discontent are wasted, not lived in the now, but instead inside the past or a conjured future. Gratitude is discontent's biggest adversary.

Practice using these simple counteractive steps to stop the theft and regain the minutes these bandits attempt to seize from you. Use their own enemies against them.

- Prevent remorse and regret with forgiveness of others and yourself.

- Eliminate worry by focusing on facts, not hypotheticals; see only the what is of today, not the what if of tomorrow.

- Avoid frustration using tolerance, acceptance, and patience.

- Dissolve hatred with love and compassion.

- Shun anger with understanding and consideration.

- Destroy discontent with gratitude.

Lilly Rocks

Sometimes life offers us great BIG lessons, in small, subtle ways. My golden retriever, Tucker, weighed more than 110 pounds in his prime. Every day without fail, he would bring those whom he admired most a large, heavy rock upon their entrance into our backyard. Those who visited often became accustomed to this unusual greeting and learned to watch their toes because he would, with love, predictably drop these small boulders directly on the recipient's foot. You might say we all learned to take his loving gestures for "granite."

Sometimes, if you were relaxing inside the house when Tucker was outside, he would drop his "catch of the day" onto the wood of the deck, resulting in a startling noise. The first few weeks of this, we would actually investigate the sound, but in time we learned to recognize the familiar thud.

My smallest dog, Lilly, only weighed twelve pounds when soaking wet, and she was Tucker's biggest fan. She idolized him and watched every move he made. Some say a dog's face is incapable of showing emotion, but I beg to differ. More than once, I'd witnessed her little face light up and her eyes widen when he entered a room. When he would lie down, she would take every opportunity to give him "kisses" while he was on her level. When he would arise, she would stand as tall as she could under his chin, desperately trying to get his attention. Though he seemed to not be bothered by her company and companionship, unfortunately, Lilly never really entered his radar.

I've always been fascinated at the friendships animals create with one another and the affection and attachment that develop as a result. Over time, I began to watch Lilly as she would intently observe Tucker. I noticed that after a while, she began to mimic Tucker's unique rock habit. She would quietly venture out to the back of the yard where the "best" rocks apparently congregated and attempt with all her might to bring back a large rock, similar to those Tucker would deem as most worthy. (I don't know what qualities a rock would have to possess to be chosen from the others, but for reasons unknown, he would literally "shop" the rocks before choosing a favorite.) Many times, after Tucker would drop a large rock, Lilly would, with the determination of a beaver building an oversized dam on a tight deadline, attempt to pick up and carry his discarded trophy. But to her dismay, her open mouth only had the circumference of a small plum, and she could never complete the mission. She would return obviously disappointed, discouraged and rockless.

As time went on, I watched and learned as an obvious life lesson displayed itself right before me in the form of a ball of black and white fur with unrelenting big round eyes and weighing less than that of a bowling ball. Lilly, in all her infinite wisdom, learned to adapt and overcome. She began to find and retrieve what I now affectionately call "Lilly Rocks." To this day, she succeeds in inconspicuously bringing back, at regular intervals, little rocks—just as she had watched Tucker do repeatedly on a larger scale through the years. Each of her small prizes is bigger than a pebble, yet smaller than a baby's fist . . . just big enough to fit in her mouth and not too heavy for her to transport with little effort through the yard and up the stairs.

Daily, I find these small rocks on the floor throughout my home. They are in my bathroom. They are in my living room. They are here in my office. I have begun to consider them small, yet significant, strategically placed reminders that I should follow Lilly's example and take life in small portions. I have learned that I can meet problems and dilemmas head on, even if they appear to me in the size of boulders—if I remember not to bite off more than I can chew at one time. I have learned to learn: I have learned to learn my limitations and to accept my life's troubles in Lilly-rock sizes and stop trying to take them on all at once. This way, I can confront and overcome them more efficiently and with the investment of far less stress.

There is a quote I've often referred to in my speeches and stories: "Life is hard . . . yard by yard. Inch by inch? It's a cinch!" Now, I have rewritten that concept as I continually tell myself and others to "Take life in Lilly rocks . . ." When life presents itself to you in boulders, take it piece by piece. Focus primarily on what you can do presently and not everything else that will follow. Consider each task as a whole component, rather than a part of the total product. In this way, you are able to accomplish small goals regularly in pursuit of the larger one, building confidence and inspiring perseverance.

> *"The secret of getting ahead is getting started. The secret of getting started is breaking your complex overwhelming tasks into small manageable tasks, and then starting on the first one."*
> —Mark Twain

Relish

So often a poem or story I write is illustrated perfectly, and often inspired, by a simple or common event. I sat writing at my desk one day and soon found myself in deep contemplation. I turned my head for a moment and stared blankly down at the floor, probably in an attempt to untangle an inspiration I was trying to convey. I caught some movement from the corner of my eye and glanced over at our cat, Wednesday. (My daughter is in charge of naming our animals . . .) She had found a strip of sunshine originating from the window on this cold and blustery day. I watched her in fascination as she literally absorbed all it had to offer. To savor something to this extent, I knew, she knew, that it was only a temporary occurrence. She writhed in its warmth and was obviously delighted with what she had discovered while walking innocently across the floor. She would shut her eyes and extend her paws so they stretched to what appeared to be their limits. She turned on her back to feel the heat the warm rays of sunshine had left on the floor. I found myself smiling and enjoying her afternoon treasure along with her. I wondered how many things I pass by in haste every day that I could stop and relish instead.

RELISH

To slow down enough to enjoy . . .
to appreciate, delight in . . . and savor;
to relish is to distinguish a difference
between eating and tasting the flavor.

Abundant, yet elusive;
life's moments are here for the taking.
But they cannot be detained,
shackled or chained;
they are memories still in the making.

Through endless tasks and errands,
our vision becomes obscured,
until we no longer see,
that each day should be
truly lived and not endured.

The days seem to pass in clusters;
as time, in rhythm, marches on . . .
by the time we realize they were here,
they are then, forever gone.

Take time to relish all the moments;
to laugh, to love, to live
to smile, to cry, to release, to embrace,
to share, to take, to give.

Consider life a dry, yet porous sponge
that will absorb, expand and grow;
let blessings fill each hollow space
until they overflow.

ON
LEGACY

Live Your Dash.

THE OTHER SIDE

I marvel at technology…
how far it has advanced,
and I wonder what our future holds;
what is next to be enhanced?

Will we someday tread upon
distant faraway grounds,
venturing above and way beyond
our limits and our bounds

to a place where no one living
has every really seen, or gone
where loved ones' souls await us
as without them, we live on?

What would I do; what would I say
if I was still alive
when, and if,
that glorious day
should miraculously arrive?

You wouldn't look the same to me,
for your death was a rebirth;
gone forever, the shell
that housed your soul
when you walked upon the earth.

But I would sense your presence
from this reunion overdue,

No matter how you might appear to me
I know
I'd know
it's you.

First, I'd tell you that I love you
in case you left with any doubt
and if I could, I'd hug your neck
in an embrace I've dreamt about

And then . . .
I would ask questions,
absorbing every word you'd say
about all that I have wondered
since the day you went away.

Can you touch? And taste?
And feel? And love?
Are your senses still intact?
Would you feel a gentle kiss
upon your cheek?
Could we interact?

Has it been a wondrous journey
since you drew your last breath,
no longer feeling pain or sorrow . . .
insusceptible to death?

Are you now invisible?
What holds your spirit and your soul?
Is your name engraved in golden script
on the angels' sacred scroll?

Are you a brilliant light that shines
your own iridescent rays,

no longer pacing your presence
on minutes, hours and days?

Have the confines and restrictions
of dates, deadlines and clocks
been replaced by golden doors
with no handles, keys or locks?

Do you . . . can you feel emotion;
sometimes joyful . . . sometimes sadder?
Do you wake at dawn
and sleep at dusk,
or does time even matter?

Would reliving all the times we've spent
and hours we've enjoyed
help ease my aching, breaking heart
and fill this empty void?

Or would it painfully exhume
the hurt I've buried deep inside
if by chance, or miracle,
your world, and mine, collide?

Would I feel whole once again;
reclaim my stance upon life's grid,
and replace the piece of my life's puzzle
that disappeared the day you did?

Someday, it will all make sense;
where I am,
and where've you've been,
when, on this side, or the other
we are together once again.

The Mourning After

I am exposed to the subject of death and dying as much as any coroner or funeral director. I am the author of "The Dash" poem. Though, as I've mentioned, I wrote this poem to reflect life, more than death, its eventual association was inevitable. My poem and funerals (celebrations of life) are now as closely linked as life and death.

Through the years, my journey as the author of "The Dash" has made me a far more realistic person. Though comprised of simple words, the poem has served as a catalyst through which I would unknowingly meet and conquer my own fears of death. Every day, without exception, I wake to a voice mail, an e-mail, or a post on my blog in which someone is sharing the story of a loved one's dash with me. Through the experiences of others, I have learned about grief and mourning, and I have learned to further appreciate the gift of time and of life.

Much like everything else in life, until I experienced death and bereavement myself, I could sympathize, but not fully empathize, with my readers. Not until I watched closely as death efficiently performed its duties on a loved one of mine, did I fully recognize the impact of the finality and the significance of the mourning after. One hour he was here, the next he was gone forever. In an instant, one life ends, and one will is never the same. The concept of the instant transition from life to death is still nearly impossible for me to fathom. It continues to intrigue me and influences the themes in many of my writings.

When I began receiving correspondence regularly about the end of so many dashes, I started to feel more like a counselor than an author. I felt a yearning to offer positive feedback and comfort to those who had formed a temporary virtual kinship with me by sharing their stories. It seemed a responsibility had been placed at my doorstep, and it was one I could not ignore. However, in order to become more helpful and compassionate in my responses, I needed to do some research to learn more about the stages of grief, responses to loss, and the steps to recovery. It seemed to me the experts had it all figured out.

Denial, anger, bargaining, depression, and acceptance. Those are the five most commonly referenced stages of grief. Although many experts insist that you must go through each stage in order to heal, I feel that each individual has his or her own personal coping mechanisms. Grieving should be as individual as the lives we live. The grieving process is comparable to a roller coaster, with sudden, unexpected ups and downs, highs and lows. If we learn not to brace ourselves against the inevitable emergence of emotions, and instead move with them and succumb to the feelings they summon, the ride will be a lot easier to endure. Temporarily indulge yourself. Use up the tears until the well runs dry. Many experience a textbook reaction after suffering a loss and follow the stages of grief in succession. Some display only three out of five. Everyone is different. Death causes feelings of loss that are so encompassing, so mind-boggling, so numbingly heart-wrenching, they can leave a black hole in your soul if you let them. The one common denominator of grief is pain, and the best remedy for easing that pain is time. Time is the salve that helps close the wound. However, there is no medicine available that will remove the scar. That is because, if the scar is erased, it will take with it, the memories.

Now, to those with whom I correspond about "The Dash," I offer the things that helped me personally through the grieving process: Lose the denial. Don't remain perpetually in the shock phase. Allow yourself to experience the pain, because it hurts, and it hurts for a reason. The longer you postpone absorbing the pain, the longer it will take you to accept the reality. Face your feelings. Bring 'em on. It happened. Nothing you can do will change the past. The sun will rise tomorrow, and you must find a way to rise with it. Do not suppress your emotions. Express your feelings. Those who do not understand the unpredictability of your current emotional state are not worthy of the label *friend*. Physically, you must move on immediately, because life must go on. However, move on emotionally only when you know you're ready. The most important thing to remember is that this intense pain will not be here forever. Remind yourself that you can endure almost anything if you know for certain that it is only temporary. Time is a great healer. I won't lie and say that time heals the pain completely. You will still feel the hurt after time passes. Yet, like a bee sting, the severe initial pain lessens, and what remains becomes more of a bearable ache, a unique longing. Tenderness and loving memories begin to fill the emptiness in your heart until it no longer becomes a place you avoid. Memories and mental visits become more pleasing than upsetting. Life does go on.

Concentrate on the legacy your loved one has left behind. A legacy of love, laughter, and the particulars of his or her dash are yours to remember, to cherish, and to keep alive. Don't turn off the light in your memory that represents a life because it is no longer here. Let it shine on forever. Use this time to focus on your own legacy too, and consider what you may someday leave behind for others. Realize that your actions today are what will be remembered tomorrow. You are the author of the story of your life. Make it a bestseller!

Live Your Dash.

REMEMBER ME

It's been a while since I left you
and I know you bear a heavy heart.
For years we were the best of friends
and in your eyes, we're now apart.

Though it may be true my idle feet
no longer tread the grounds of earth,
it is you who can truly justify
what the steps they took are worth.

Realize now that I am only gone
if you choose for me to be . . .
if you hesitate to speak my name
or recall each memory.

If you reject the image of my face
because it brings you pain,
then my life, my love, my laughter
will all have been in vain.

I know you miss my presence
from the steady tears upon your face,
but these tears you cry are not for me,
for I am in a better place.

I am no longer suffering.
I feel no pain, nor have I sorrow.
I've gone forward to this beautiful place
to spend today and every tomorrow.

So laugh at our jokes, remember our time
and freely speak my name.
If you'll relive our years together,
then it won't be an end that came.

Embrace the things we've shared;
revisit places we have been.
Keep me alive within your heart
and I will never die again.

Yes, it's true that it won't be the same
and the same . . . it will never be,
but I will always be by your side
if you will always remember me.

Is That You?

I wrote the poem "Is That You?" to illustrate my belief in the possibility that our lost loved ones occasionally send us "signs" to let us know they are still, in some distant way, a part of our lives. Maybe it's just the optimist in my soul, or maybe it stems from an inherent desire to never completely let go of the relationships I've had with friends and family who have since moved on.

A perfect example of this concept is this photo. My dad, who passed away several years ago, loved to fish. It was more than a hobby for him; it was his life's passion. Last year, during a visit with a friend to a butterfly sanctuary, I began a conversation about the "signs" I desperately wanted to believe my father was sending to me after his passing. My friend was intrigued by this thought process, but I did not feel completely convinced. After all, it could sound a bit far-fetched to some. As soon as I'd uttered the words, "I think we should at least remain open to this idea, should a sign appear to us," I turned to see this butterfly perfectly perched on the branch above me. I quickly grabbed my camera to see if I could capture the moment and prove to myself that what my mind's eye had convinced me I was viewing had indeed been there. I also wanted a picture to show others, as I was curious to find out if my friends and family could discover in this scene what I had. Look carefully at the tip of the butterfly's wing to the left of the photo . . . do you see the head of a fish? Some see it, some do not.

Possibly a coincidence. Probably a fluke. Either way, it brought me solace and comfort that day to believe that maybe . . . just maybe, my favorite fisherman is still close by.

IS THAT YOU?

We suffer and we grieve
when we lose someone who we love
and it brings us comfort to believe
they've been called from up above.

But often times I'll wonder
in the things I do and see
if somehow they're trying to let me know
that they are watching over me.

I believe more each day
that flukes occurring just by chance
don't happen by coincidence,
or by simple happenstance.

And I'll find myself wondering
if each incident is a clue,
or if I should dare to consider asking
the question, "Is That You?"

Is that you in the vivid flower
standing in the midst of weeds and grass
or in the multi-colored prism reflected
from the light upon my glass?

Is that you in the ray of sunshine
I feel warm upon my back
or in the most brilliant star that shines
as the sky fades into black?

Is that you in the whirlpool of autumn leaves
captured by the breeze
or in the single leaf that will grace my path
as I walk beneath the trees?

Is that you in the sign that suddenly appears
when it seems I've lost my way,
or in the strip of clear blue sky
peering through clouds of stormy gray?

Is that you in the lone butterfly
that appears before its season
or in the smile of a passing stranger
that I receive without a reason?

These occasions have begun
to somehow calm my sorrow and fear.
For though you're gone, they may be your way
of showing me that you're still near.

Boxes

I started cleaning out a back closet one day, and on the top rack, I found three large boxes. I recognized them instantly and drew in a slow, deep breath as I brought them down from the shelf on which they'd spent the last five years undisturbed. I carefully pulled back the tape that I distinctly remembered applying on the day I brought these boxes home. I recalled the tears that fell under the strips of tape as I pressed them slowly along the corners and seams of each box to securely hold them together until I was ready to open them again and, with a clearer mind, inspect their contents. I thought how ironic it was that this product was called "masking tape" as I had certainly tried to "mask" my feelings that day by attempting, unsuccessfully, to seal my hurt and pain inside each box as well.

I opened the first box and began to carefully sift through the black and white photos, documents, and papers. My eye caught the corner of a sheet of paper I recognized as being written in my handwriting. As I removed it from the box and began to read, I realized it was a poem I'd written to my father when I was thirteen years old. In it, I'd referred to a favorite joke of his:

"Daddy, I know it must be hard . . . seeing your little girl grow up. Telling everyone you know, that you've raised me from a pup!"

I grinned as I recalled the amusement in his voice every time he had repeated that little joke. I remember staying up late one night, writing that poem and leaving it for him in his lunch box so he would open it and read it at work the next day. I wondered now how often he had reread it over the thirty years he'd saved it. Then I looked back into the box. I glanced at his passport, some silver dollars and lapel pins from his employer marking ten- and twenty-year milestones. I found an old fishing license, some bills, receipts, birthday cards, and letters.

I stared intently at a photo I'd taken of him about a month before he had passed away. I asked myself how it happened that seventy-four years of walking this Earth could eventually be contained within three boxes. Then, it occurred to me, that what my father had actually left behind was so much more than anyone could place in any box. Even if it were possible: if love, guidance, support, and protection were tangible items, there could never be a box enormous enough to house all that he had given to me.

The items in these boxes contained a paper trail that began in 1930 and ended in 2004. From their contents, anyone who hadn't known him would be able to ascertain his financial status, how many children he had, where he had traveled, different residences throughout his life, but not what truly made him the man he was.

I realized then that what was in these boxes didn't truly matter. What mattered most in my father's legacy were the things I still carry with me every day: the life lessons I still hear in his words repeated aloud in my mind, the respect he demanded I show others, the love and affection I feel free to give my children, the humor I find even in the most difficult situations, and the empathy for others I feel in my heart when I see someone who is suffering.

Those are a few examples of the "things" my father left me. Maybe that's why such things are meant to be intangible. If they were physical objects that we could see and hold, they might very well be sealed into boxes and put high upon a shelf to be revisited every five years or so, instead of being remembered and utilized every single day, literally inside the soul of a still living, breathing being.

After going through the boxes, I'd found that I was not yet ready to discard their contents, and probably never would be. So, I resealed them and put them back in the closet. Yet, this time, I placed them on a low, visible shelf as a reminder to me, a reminder of the most important lesson my father taught me: that I should strive to live a life that ensures my own legacy is more than a monetary inheritance to someday be divvied up amongst my loved ones; a life that ensures that what I leave behind will instead be carried in the hearts and memories of those I knew and loved, as a very important part of their own lives.

That day I vowed to leave my loved ones and friends with so much more than what can be packed up and sealed . . . into boxes.

I do not dwell on dying,
nor do I look forward to the day,
but I do not want my eulogy
to read like my résumé!

It shall not boast accomplishments;
it shall not, my life, exalt
by exaggerating all my strengths
and concealing every fault.

The listeners there each knew me well
and loved me, just because.
They are all my friends and family
so . . . tell it like it was!

Tomorrow's Eve

My second grader taught me a valuable lesson many years ago shortly after the holidays. I had finished work one day in January and went to ASP (which stands for After School Program, though the children often refer to it as "After School Prison") to pick her up, go home, and begin the wondrous task of selecting something I hadn't defrosted earlier to make for dinner. I routinely signed my name on the roster and sat in the nearby designated chair, which was still warm from my ASP parent predecessors who had, exhausted from a day's work, waited there before selecting one of the hyper children from the pack to take home that evening, hoping they had chosen the right one. Like robots we took our turn claiming the little humans that belonged to us, attempting to hide our tired minds with a perky greeting and a genuinely interested, "So, how was school today?" attitude.

My daughter came out of the library doors with a smile upon her face, as usual. She gave me a high-five, a hug, and her twenty-pound book bag to lug to the car. We buckled up our seat belts, and while I began to absorb her interpretation of all the important events of elementary school in the form of "Megan said that . . . " and "Bradley did this," I began to back out of the parking space. Out of the blue, I heard my daughter say, "Hey mom, let's not go home." To which I replied, "Silly girl, we have to go home. Mommy has to finish last night's dishes, make dinner, and finish the laundry—and I'm sure you have lots of homework to do." She thought about the assignments Mrs. Carlin had given them that afternoon and repeated with renewed conviction, "Let's not go home . . . let's go to the park and then go for ice cream . . . let's celebrate!!" I said, "Sweetheart, the holidays are over. There is no reason to celebrate now. We have to wait until next year to celebrate again." The honesty and innocence of her reply will forever remain in my mind, "Mommy, we don't need a reason to celebrate. Let's be happy we're together today. Let's make it our own holiday, and we'll call it, 'Tomorrow's Eve.'"

Immediately, my suspicious mind started questioning her intent. Had she really had this wonderful idea, or was it just a clever disguise to get what she wanted? After all, she was an expert on how to manipulate me using the Working Mommy Guilt technique. Wasn't it just last year she used her highly polished WMG skills to make us the proud parents of "Cookie," the perpetually excavating guinea pig? Either way, I was thoroughly impressed with her thought process. We were stopped at the intersection by then, ready to make our routine left turn to drive home. The park, of course, would mean a right turn. (Possibly indicating some subliminal message that turning *right* was the *right* thing to do? Now, how did she do that? She *is* good!) My mind searched for an answer to give her, reasons why we could not possibly celebrate "Tomorrow's Eve" today. I knew every reason I thought of, however, would be skillfully debated and overruled. It was like dealing with an overzealous defense attorney. I looked into her big blue eyes. I thought of the dishes, the laundry, and the "busyness" that awaited me at home. The moment didn't require words. I switched the turn signal from left to right, and we went on to celebrate our first "Tomorrow's Eve." We played tag. I went down the slide in my business suit and heels. Then we ate ice cream. That day I left her much more than what could be packed into boxes someday.

Make the time to schedule more "Tomorrow's Eve" holidays on your busy calendar, and celebrate them each, with passion!

WE COULD CELEBRATE THE JOY OF LIVING

BY CHOOSING TO BELIEVE

THAT ANY DAY CAN BE A HOLIDAY

IF WE OBSERVE, TOMORROW'S EVE . . .

Names

I've always wanted someone to make my name the password required to access his or her computer. For some reason, I began to consider the act of being designated as a computer password some sort of twenty-first century rite of passage or a type of modern honor one person could bestowed upon another. To my knowledge, no one ever has, but there is still time!

Our name, when spoken by our loved ones or those with whom our paths have crossed, instantly brings to mind certain adjectives, along with a specific "aura" created from memories and interactions. Are your life's actions living up to the adjectives you'd want others to associate with your name? Your name is more than just a title; words printed on your social security card; and a combination of consonants and vowels that, when spoken aloud, make you turn your head in an immediate, habitual response. You are responsible for ensuring that your name is more than just a label that you were given at birth.

Your name when brought to the forefront of a conversation, not only brings forth virtual photos of your face and your person, but also is immediately connected with particular images, thoughts, and ideals that have been subconsciously "assigned" to you by your friends, loved ones, and those with whom you have associated. It is entirely up to you to decide what you want those thoughts to be and to conduct yourself daily so that your actions and words are parallel to all that you want your name to bring to mind.

For example, I think about the images and adjectives linked to the words *Linda Ellis* in the minds and memories of those who have been a part of my life's journey thus far. What they are for certain, I may never know, but what I want them to be, I do know. My goal is to live my dash so that the repetition of the syllables in my name calls for a smile. I want the person speaking my name to associate it with lightness, freedom, and undeniable benevolence. If I haven't virtually etched those images into the sounds that comprise my name, I have not been working hard enough to reach that goal.

Your name, as spoken, and as remembered, represents more than your reputation. Through the years, it becomes an embodiment of the ways in which you have lived your dash, and touched others' lives. Live your life in such a manner that when you imagine your name being spoken in your absence, there will never be a desire to be present to defend it.

KEEP YOUR NAME FREE OF SHAME,

LET ITS SPIRIT NOT BE DEMOLISHED . . .

FOR IF YOU WANT YOUR "SELF" TO SHINE,

YOU'VE GOT TO KEEP IT POLISHED!

The Sole Soul

Born and raised in a small, friendly southern town, an old man spent most of his adult life on Earth worrying about making, investing, and counting his money. His only acquaintances—purposely—were business partners or fellow investors, and the only family members who came to see him did so in order to someday secure a prominent place in his will.

At eighty-two years of age, he passed away, probably peacefully they say, in his chair. He was positioned in that chair four or five days, per the coroner's reports, before he was discovered. The only reason he was found then was because of a neighbor's unleashed dogs continuously barking outside his front door.

He lived his life building barriers. He wore an invisible armor between him and the world. If a person did not fill a financial purpose or offer the promise of profit, he or she was of no use to him. His heart was cold. He had never allowed himself to experience the thrill of falling in love, the warmth of holding an infant in his arms, or the joys of life found outside the realm of diversified portfolios and profit and loss statements.

He had built walls that protected his soul, his home, and his heart from anyone who might get close enough to cause him pain. He knew this as a foolproof way to prevent hurt and, by doing so, denied himself love, companionship, and friendship. He knew any relationships of the heart involved exposure, vulnerability, and risk, and the only risks he vowed he would ever take were in the stock market. He could risk investing his fortune but would not chance his heart.

When the old man learned he was terminally ill, he paid a visit to his attorney to get his affairs into order. As a practical matter, he took a drive to the local cemetery to select and purchase a grave site. He walked the farthest distance south from the last purchased grave in a particular row, then turned and walked fifty yards facing east. It was the very last site in which the cemetery was permitted to bury. There, he had convinced himself, was the perfect location for his remains to spend eternity, after his sole soul had left his body.

It was a dark, rainy day when he was placed into the ground. No one was there with a kind word to say. No mournful tears fell upon his casket before he was lowered into his eternal resting place. The temporary tents the cemetery personnel had constructed shielded no mourners in black suits and black dresses from the rain that fell. No words of prayer were spoken. His assets were his legacy, left behind and divided among an eager and receptive group of distant nieces and nephews.

For two years, his wishes were fulfilled. His body spent this time away from others, just as he had planned. But, as progress would have it, the county decided to build a three-lane highway heading southeast of the cemetery. The owners of the cemetery had reached financial hardships and were eager to negotiate. They bargained every piece of unused land out to the very border of their property. The county was permitted an easement of twenty feet from the last grave site. The project took months to complete. Heavy machinery, smoke, dust, and noise extinguished the silence and serenity surrounding the area he had chosen for his shell to spend eternity.

The invisible fence he had attempted to construct around his gravestone cannot block the dirt and pebbles that ricochet off cars and trucks as they travel down this busy road today. Now considered an icon for loneliness, each passerby has a clear view of his bland gray headstone as they speed by en route to their destinations, and many of them wonder, as I do, about the headstone, standing alone in such close proximity to the pavement.

We cannot separate ourselves from the rest of the world, because we are each a part of everything. We are connected through the air we breathe, the ground upon which we walk and everything our senses absorb. We are never alone, neither were we designed to be. We are meant to be a part of everything, and everything, a part of us. We are intended to leave footprints on this Earth and fingerprints on the lives we touch.

Live Your Dash.

NOBODY CAME

Soaked with sweat and filled with fear,
he rose quickly in his bed.
The dream he'd had the night before
so real inside his head.

Every image, every emotion,
the night's hours left behind
were clear as crystal in his memory,
forever engraved upon his mind.

He could still see his lifeless body,
a silken pillow 'neath his head . . .
what should have been a room of mourners
was an empty room, instead.

No one to stand, no one to speak,
no words of love, no prayers.
No flowers with cards of sympathy.
Just empty tables, empty chairs.

The details of those scenes;
his body cold and all alone . . .
the realization that nobody came
chilled him to the bone.

How could this have happened?
Not one person came to grieve?
Of all the people in my life,
was no one sad to see me leave?

Were all my years a waste of time?
Did my life not have worth?
Were there no hearts or lives I touched?
Did I leave no footprint here on earth?

What could be the reasons why
nobody cared, nobody came?
But in his heart, he knew the answer;
he only had himself to blame.

Though a dream is not reality.
It made him stop and think.
In the chain of human kindness,
had he been the weakest link?

He vowed today to start anew,
to stop fretting and complaining,
to touch a life and make a difference
with every day he had remaining.

To change the way he lives his life
so that each day will include
an act of kindness, thoughtful deed,
a simple show of gratitude.

To leave a legacy of kindness,
and focus on what's true and real,
trying always to remember
just how other people feel.

To make these changes happen now,
show compassion, share a smile,
for tomorrow is never guaranteed
and today is here for just a while.

And when his days have come and gone
as tears fall and flowers bloom,
a large and mournful crowd will fill
what was once an empty room.

(Special thanks to Marc Turner for his input.)

TOUCHED BY "THE DASH"

The Dash's Dash
(1996—XXXX)

HISTORY OF "THE DASH" POEM

I've used the term *The Dash's Dash* because the original creation, a unique combination of 241 words, has literally created a life of its own. Its "birth" occurred in 1996 when I wrote it, and yet the date of its demise will never be a reality. Its own life, its own "dash" is infinite, its legacy carved in stone, and it will live on long after the footprints its creator has placed on Earth have faded. Inside its simple stanzas lie the mystery and complexity of life. The poem's rhythmic message subconsciously forces readers to be suddenly keenly aware of the brevity of it all. It has touched more lives than anyone could have ever imagined, dreamed or calculated and will continue to do so for generations to come.

I've realized, that although I own the copyright to "The Dash," it's as though I no longer own the poem . . . in a way, the world does. I compare it to a seed I planted many years ago, which quickly sprouted and continues to grow exponentially, being continuously cultivated by the millions of souls inspired by its message. It is unfathomable to me the number of loving legacies, rerouted journeys, smiles worn, and tears shed as a result of my writing this work.

Timing is everything, they say. "The Dash" entered the world in a time of a technological explosion and has since become an entity unto itself. Full time, around the clock, it continues to work each day, touching lives and touching hearts. As a rational person who requires solid evidence to sway my opinion, I must admit I've come to believe in, and accept, the concept that this poem has a unique purpose and a reason for its creation and existence. Maybe propelled by a higher power, maybe by a force of nature or maybe by sheer coincidence, but how else can one explain its enormous effect on the world having been originated by one woman without the wherewithal or resources at the time to launch such an explosive inspiration into the world? I was busy living my own dash while the poem was out working its magic. It took me many years, and countless stories of this inspiration reaching the lives of those who need it, when they need it, to truly believe in its power. Though still bewildered, I no longer doubt its abilities or the potential of its successor, *Live Your Dash*.

I was complimented in an interview recently, in which the gentleman said, "It's very impressive where you have taken 'The Dash.'" I replied, "It's more impressive where 'The Dash' has taken me . . ."

A few years ago, I was invited to speak at the National Funeral Directors' Association Convention. Of course, it was in reference to my authorship of "The Dash" poem, as it has had a profound effect on this particular industry over the years, I'm sure more than any other. However, when I'd written this poem many years prior, I had intended it to be about life, not to focus on death. Yet, over time I began to realize to my dismay, that this work had become one of the most widely read pieces at gravesides, funerals, and "Celebrations of Life." It wasn't that I didn't feel pride that so many were finding solace in my words, I simply questioned whether the writing's intent was being misconstrued.

I knew this speaking engagement would be a wonderful opportunity, but I must admit I was hesitant to accept the invitation initially. Though more comfortable with the subject of death than I had been in previous years, due largely in part to those with whom I'd traded correspondence about their personal experiences regarding "The Dash" poem, I wondered what being in the company of hundreds of funeral directors would require of me, emotionally.

My concerns were soon put to rest when I met so many of the warm, caring, and wonderful directors personally and heard the stories of how my words had affected literally thousands of people who had attended events at their facilities. Humbled, I listened carefully to each story as I was even more convinced of the power of this special group of words to touch hearts and change lives. I reflected on how strange and wonderful a feeling it was to learn how perfect strangers and their families were being moved so by my words. Again, it occurred to me that lives were literally being changed and journeys altered due to an inspiration I'd written at my desk one day.

What occurred to me most was that "The Dash" poem was being used at these celebrations, not only to reflect upon the "dash" of the deceased, but also to enlighten the family and friends of those in attendance. The poem was not at all a "funeral poem" as I had now begun to consider it myself. It was indeed being used to represent life, as I had originally intended!

Yes, the poem is used to symbolize the little dash of those whose days on Earth have ended. But I realized then, that it also has the ability to alter the lives of those left to live many more, by influencing them to cherish and appreciate each, having now been "Touched by 'The Dash'." Throughout the years, I've received thousands of calls, letters, and e-mail messages containing stories from those whose lives have been touched by the words of "The Dash." I have chosen some of my favorites to share with you . . .

THOUGH WE ALL MAY STRIVE TO PROSPER

DURING OUR TIME HERE ON EARTH,

IT ISN'T THE MONEY IN OUR BANK ACCOUNT

THAT MEASURES WHAT OUR DASH IS WORTH.

The Original
"The Dash"

Live Your Dash.

The Dash

I read of a man who stood to speak
at the funeral of a friend.
He referred to the dates on her tombstone
from the beginning . . . to the end.

He noted that first came the date of her birth
and spoke of the following date with tears,
but he said what mattered most of all
was the dash between those years.

For that dash represents all the time
that she spent alive on earth
and now only those who loved her
know what that little line is worth.

For it matters not, how much we own,
the cars . . . the house . . . the cash.
What matters is how we live and love
and how we spend our dash.

So think about this long and hard,
are there things you'd like to change?
For you never know how much time is left
that can still be rearranged.

If we could just slow down enough
to consider what's true and real
and always try to understand
the way other people feel.

And be less quick to anger
and show appreciation more
and love the people in our lives
like we've never loved before.

If we treat each other with respect
and more often wear a smile,
remembering that this special dash
might only last a little while.

So when your eulogy is being read
with your life's actions to rehash,
would you be proud of the things they say
about how you spent your dash?

David Cook

L ast year, I received an e-mail from a fan of recording artist and talented former *American Idol* winner, David Cook. She had included a photo, stating that it had a connection to one of my writings. I was intrigued, so I opened the attachment. To my surprise and delight, there it was, the entire last stanza of my poem, "The Dash," designed as a striking tattoo inked upon the left forearm of David Cook! I was aware of David's musical talents as I had been an avid fan of *American Idol* and had watched with delight as he won the

seventh season competition in 2008. I remembered the story of his success, in particular, because he didn't intend to try out for the show initially. He was there, instead, to lend support to his youngest brother. However, during the course of auditions, David chose to try out as well and was selected to move forward through the competition, eventually being voted the winner.

And just one week after winning the *American Idol* competition, David Cook rewrote chart history with a record-breaking fourteen debuts on Billboard's Hot Digital Songs chart. He also had eleven songs jump onto Billboard's Hot 100 chart, which was the highest number of new entries in a single week by an artist since the Beatles in 1964. His *American Idol* coronation song, "The Time of My Life," held the #1 position at mainstream AC radio for nearly four months straight and has the honor of being not only the biggest single debut, but also the highest selling coronation single in the history of *American Idol*, and has been certified platinum.

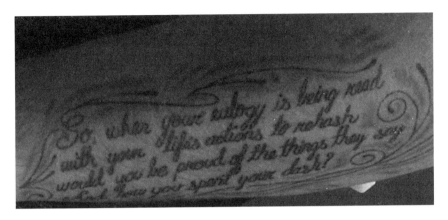

While learning of his accomplishments and accolades, I learned more about David Cook, the man. The more I read, the more I realized how well the tattoo epitomized the way in which he lives his life and the more proud I became knowing he had chosen my poem to carry with him every day. He seemed to be a humble, grateful young man with his feet firmly planted on the ground and his priorities in order. I then watched *American Idol*'s "Idol Gives Back" segment, and my pride was reaffirmed as I watched the footage of his recent trip to Ethiopia. His genuine empathy and compassion for the plight of young women there shone through in his interviews. I purposely focused on the tattoo on his arm and thought how my thoughts and words had gone with him and inspired him as he traveled with the UN Foundation to help educate and empower women of that region. What a wonderful, fulfilling way to be spending part of your dash, David!

"So when your eulogy is being read

with your life's actions to rehash,

would you be proud of the things they say

about how you spent your dash?"

Senator Bob Dole

A while ago, I received an e-mail about "The Dash" poem that caught my attention, particularly as it contained a link to a C-SPAN video recording of a recent National Press Club Meeting regarding the Treatment and Care of Wounded Veterans, a subject close to my heart.

The unique thing about this video was that former U.S. Senator, Senate Republican Leader, and 1996 presidential nominee Bob Dole was reading aloud my words! As the keynote speaker for the event, he had chosen my poem to illustrate and convey a notion that he and I share . . . debt and gratitude for our wounded veterans. Not only was he reading my poem with obvious emotion, but also he prefaced his recitation with the words: "We owe these young men and women everything . . ."

Simultaneously proud, humbled, and amazed, I literally shook my head in disbelief. As I listened to him begin the seventh stanza, specifically the lines: "And be less quick to anger . . . and show appreciation more . . . and love the people in our lives . . . like we've never loved before," there was no mistaking the emotions my words brought forth in this man. I stared, almost bewildered, at my computer monitor. Had the words I'd written years ago actually touched this combat veteran? This man who had been struck by enemy shrapnel while trying to drag his wounded comrade into a shell hole? This man who had received two Bronze Stars for his "heroism under fire"? I recall the realization of how something intangible, such as words, when combined in a specific, unique pattern, can have the power to reach directly through to someone's heart and ignite emotion. I remember thinking there was some sort of ironic, conflicting comparison between the lead pellets that had pierced this man physically during wartime and my words that seemed to pierce him emotionally now.

As I learned more about Bob Dole, I wondered if my words had also inspired him during any of his various humanitarian efforts. I like to think they had.

I wrote to Senator Bob Dole to thank him, let him know how proud I was that he'd chosen my poem to recite to our veterans, and ask if I could include him in my book. I received this letter in response:

SENATOR BOB DOLE

THE ATLANTIC BUILDING 950 F STREET, N.W., 10TH FLOOR
WASHINGTON, D.C. 20004

January 26, 2011

Linda Ellis
1050 E. Piedmont Road
Suite E-135
Marietta, GA 30062

Dear Linda:

Thank you for your letter and for including me in your book. I am now recuperating from knee surgery and other health problem [sic], but getting better each day. Below are my thoughts, and please let me know if you need anything further.

"In speaking to audiences all over the country and beyond, over many, many years and on any number of different occasions, it has always been evident that there are certain things that touch people the same way regardless of their position, status, political affiliation, or any other criteria. What seems to me to be universal is the desire to reflect upon life's true meaning, the need to appreciate our lives and the love of family and friends, and there is an innate longing to do all we can do to contribute and utilize our talents. The common thread for people everywhere seems to me to have been a yearning for the truths and values that endure from over time, regardless of generation.

I was handed Linda Ellis' poem "The Dash" several years ago, and pretty soon after I took to reading it aloud to audiences gathered for any and all reasons. I believe it captures the spirit of our journey and those universal desires. I cannot count the folks who have heard me read who have been touched, who either asked for a copy, or came up to me to comment about how it inspired them. In short, it was a reminder to live our lives with all we've got, appreciate the blessings we've been given, and do everything possible to make our time on earth meaningful.

In recent months I've spent a considerable time at Walter Reed Army Medical Center, both as a patient and additionally meeting the great men and women who serve our country and make enormous sacrifices. That experience has been another reminder of "the dash" in life that Linda Ellis has encouraged people to live, a perspective on life captured not only in her poem but embodied in people like these true heroes. They are fathers and mothers, sisters ad brothers, friends and colleagues who inspire me and others by the way they live, by what they accomplish, and by the courage and conviction with which they approach each day."

Thank you and good luck with you [sic] new endeavors.

God Bless America,

Bob Dole

Tim Currier

My name is Tim Currier. I am the Massena Basketball Association Commissioner and I also am the Junior Varsity Boys Basketball Coach. I'm the Chief of Police of our community here in Massena, New York (on the Canadian border). Last year I read "The Dash" poem at our twenty-fifth annual basketball tournament celebration, and it was incredibly received. Later in the year, the Board of Directors created "The Dash" Award and presented it to me because of my work with the program for nearly twenty-three years. The person who created the award said, "When I heard you read that poem, I knew exactly how to honor you." I am so honored by the award and privileged to have your poem attached to it. Linda, I cannot tell you how inspiring your poem is to me. There is no piece that I have found that comes close to your poem in reflecting how a person's life matters. [Below is the text of "The Dash" Award given to Tim Currier.]

Massena Basketball Association's
"The Dash" Award, 2006
Presented to . . .
Tim J. Currier, Chief of Police, Messena, New York

For your dedication and leadership toward advancing the game of basketball for the youth of the Massena area.

The time and leadership you have given to the Massena Basketball Association has provided great stability to the organization that will last for generations to come.

This unselfish time is part of the character that defines how you are spending your dash. Thank you for being a part of our organization and always remember, "For it matters not, how much we own; the cars, the house, the cash. What matters is how we live and love and how we spend our dash."

—MBA Board of Directors and Friends

How "The Dash" Touched Chief Currier After He Received the Award . . . .

From the moment I read "The Dash," I said, "That's it. It can't be clearer than this." My wife and I have a nine-year-old son, and the poem summed up the way we want him to live his life. We want him to love his family, love God, and to be respectful and compassionate. In particular, I appreciate the three paragraphs that begin with "to slow down long enough to consider what's true and real."

I keep the poem in three places: It's hanging on my office wall at work next to my desk, at my home office, and I keep three paragraphs in a card in my wallet, too. I use the poem to reflect on things when they are going particularly bad, and it helps ground me sometimes. I read the words often as I hope I can inspire others as well to be compassionate, respectful, and have dignity. Dignity is important and vital to people who hold positions of public safety or public trust. It's so important we lead with integrity and dignity. Some days I have times when I want to scream, and nothing is going right. Reading the words in "The Dash" takes me down a couple of notches.

"To consider what's true and real" really simplifies everything in that one particular line of "The Dash." You then know what matters. For everyone, it's different, but for me it's my family and the more than thirty people who work for me in the police office because their lives are affected by their jobs, and, as I see it, when I affect their jobs, I affect their lives also.

It's the same thing in coaching basketball. I use this poem when I am dealing with the Junior Varsity Boy's Basketball Team I coach. You can make a difference in people's lives, and this poem is the compass on how you can make a difference. It is my moral compass. As I lead the safety of our community, I follow the words in this poem. Another way I have looked at this is by living our lives by the golden rule, which is a great standard, but what does treating others like you'd like to be treated mean? For me, "The Dash" defines the golden rule.

I hope one day my dash says that I was compassionate, respectful, and lived with honor. Most of all, the message in this poem is not just about reflecting on your life, but more importantly [about] living your life in a meaningful way.

Captain Richard Marshall

Changes in life are never easy. They move slowly and in degrees and never without storms. I remember the day I first heard the poem "The Dash." I needed to hear and read it again to understand it. Only then came the realization that it was more than just a poem. How a few words could light such a fervor within me was puzzling. I thought the poem was more like a compass, which in its own way shed a spiritual and moral beam one could follow. Yes, something I could count on for direction [on which] I could chart my future course. Long ago, I lost my faith, and when my spiritual batteries bottomed out, I lost my God, my family, friends, even my north, east, west, and south. If you don't know where you are, how can you get to anywhere? I remember thinking, "Had I reached the bottom of all bottoms; is this the end?" Then one day I met a wonderful woman who gently helped me put away my bottle and needle. A person who cared enough to save my life. Not an easy voyage through the years, but slowly my course was changing.

When my mother-in-law died, I first heard the poem "The Dash." It was read at her memorial by her son. I immediately felt a surge of spiritual warmth inside of me. "Did that little dash between birth and death have a life of its own?" I thought. Could it be an invitation to inventory a person's special skills, talents, and abilities? Could that dash reveal the excellence within a person? I recalled the day my six-year-old daughter died and started to fill in her dash in my mind. Her crystal clear essence and brightness came through even after her passing thirty-eight years ago. Then I started thinking of the Marine brothers I had lost and what courageous dashes they left for us to recall. And of course, [I think of] my cherished friends, as I sail single-handed and raise my cup while thinking of their dashes. And now, entering the last quarter of my life, I am blessed to know my family, comrades, and friends come to life as I recall our moments of life together. Yes "The Dash" HAS INDEED BECOME MY PASSPORT TO ETERNITY. I remember Jimmy Durante saying: "Goodnight Mrs. Calabash, wherever you are." Well long live "The Dash," and thank you, Linda Ellis, wherever you are.

Today I am happy and close to my family, spiritually alive, and staying on course. You may only see one person sailing *The Dasher* but believe me I've the best crew in the universe with me always. My sloop, *The Dasher*, named for the poem, "The Dash," was built in 1968 and completely restored by me from 2004 to 2005. She carries copies of "The Dash" as she glides to her many destinations. "Is your boat named for a reindeer?" people ask. "No," I say, "she is on a mission to explain the little dash between your birth and death." You also have a dash; so put your shoulder to the dash, live it well, and make it shine.

Bev Martin

Founded in January 2008, the DASH Group is an evolving community of friends who come together socially to expand upon their capabilities and resources to bring value to their community.

The goals of the members of DASH are to inspire its community of Anacortes, Washington, and to make a difference in the lives of their neighbors by utilizing their gifts of time, talent, and volunteer commitment.

The name of this group came about after viewing Linda Ellis's "The Dash" poem. Members of this group were inspired to spend their "dashes" collectively to make a difference and leave a lasting fingerprint on their community.

DASH Group projects have included adopting a family for Christmas, assisting the local Red Cross chapter, helping high school students with lunch funds, lending support to the local library with two Murder Mystery fundraisers, designing and producing four large career-center banners for the local high school career center, raising $25,000 toward rebuilding the Island Trestle (which was destroyed by fire), raising $7,700 for the local hospital, raising funds and food for the local food banks, and currently we are involved with a local high school community-service project for students.

Due to the DASH Group's positive efforts, many requests for assistance in a variety of projects are sent by community groups. When asked what "DASH" stands for, the reply is always the same: "The dash between your date of birth and your date of death is really the legacy you leave." The DASH Group is a true testament to how people may spend their dashes, with meaning and purpose.

Susan Phelps

I was so moved by the words of "The Dash" that, in 2004, I called my girlfriends to ask them to lunch. I shared the poem with them and immediately ["The]Dash" Club was born.

We have been meeting once a month since. One person is in charge of organizing and arranging the outing. She phones the members the night before and tells them only the necessary dress code and where to meet. Our outings have included visits to open gardens and vineyards, bowling, caving, go-kart racing, fox flying, and endless more adventures. Our club outings have also given us all a chance to meet new friends.

All of this because of the powerful words of "The Dash." Linda, I know you receive endless mail, but I do hope you get to read this so you know the difference you have made in our lives here on our island. I must let you know we are all over fifty.

The biggest thank you, Linda, comes from me personally. Your words were what inspired me how to spend my dash when my marriage ended after forty-three years. In one way, it was my mantra and five years on, I've managed to buy a business, build a house, and always have goals in my day. So now my cash register of life is full of dash spending. As I build my business, I think of the words and know I have full control of my DASH.

Regards,

Susan Phelps
Tasmania, Australia

Sean Kanan

Actor, The Bold and the Beautiful, General Hospital, *and currently,*
The Young and the Restless

For some time I knew that I wanted write about many of the extraordinary experiences which have shaped my life. Like most people, I have had my ups and downs. I wanted to share some of the life strategies I have learned along the way. For a guy that has always prided himself on being proactive and a go-getter, I wasn't able to get going with my book. Right around that time a dear friend of mine asked if I was familiar with Linda Ellis's poem, "The Dash." I had never heard of it, but was very eager to read the words which seemed to have so profoundly affected my friend. I remember as I read Linda's words for the first time how I felt such a sense of connection. "The Dash" reaffirms so many thoughts that I have held all of my life. I instantly felt a flow of creative energy and whispered a phrase that I had heard somewhere but cannot remember where: "Life is not a dress rehearsal."

I began to write my book, *Freeing David*, soon after. From time to time I would reread "The Dash" for a burst of inspiration. I later decided that I wanted to include Linda's beautiful words in my book to share with as many people as possible. I also decided that I wanted to try and connect with this woman whose words had given me so much. After a little investigation I found an e-mail address and wrote Linda. I was shocked and pleasantly surprised when she responded. I asked if she would read some of my book and consider writing the foreword. She graciously agreed and asked if I would contribute a few words to her new book. It occurred to me that the wonderfully strange way that we have come into one another's lives speaks to the essence of "The Dash." Linda's words serve as a constant reminder to live my life to the fullest ensuring that my dash will motivate and inspire others to do the same. Linda, thank you for your wisdom, generosity, and beautiful spirit.

With humbled sincerity,
Sean Kanan

Carol Ann Cole

arol Ann is an author, a professional speaker, and the founder of a national fund-raiser. Carol Ann and her mother Mary were diagnosed with breast cancer within days of each other. Deciding there was more to life than climbing the corporate ladder, Carol Ann walked away. Carol Ann is a Member of the Order of Canada, and she has received numerous additional awards including the Golden Jubilee Medal; the elite Maclean's Honor Role; the Terry Fox Citation of Honor; the YWCA Women's Recognition Award; the Canadian Auto Workers Woman of the Year; L'Oreal's dozen outstanding Canadians celebrating International Women's Day; and the Jewish Women International Woman of the Year. She is profiled in *Canadian Who's Who* and in the 2005 edition of *1000 Great Women of the 21st Century* published by the American Biographical Institute in Raleigh, North Carolina.

As the founder of the Comfort Heart Initiative, a national fund-raiser that has raised more than one million dollars for cancer research, Carol Ann has put hundreds of thousands of Comfort Hearts into the hands of Canadians and people around the world.

She wrote:

Early in 2001 my daughter-in-law shared "The Dash" with me. As a professional speaker, I am always seeking meaningful material that I can share with an audience. I fell in love with "The Dash" and contacted Linda Ellis immediately. I wanted to meet this incredible author and I wanted to seek her permission to use her poem in my motivational work and to publish it in my second book, *Lessons Learned Upside the Head*. I am honored to say we became fast friends.

I am a cancer survivor (twice!) and often speak with audiences who may need something personal they can hang on to—something like "The Dash." I read Linda's poem, or quote from it. Specifically, I share:

"For it matters not, how much we own,
the cars . . . the house . . . the cash.
What matters is how we live and love
and how we spend our dash."

and, without fail, my audiences relate to her words.

My third book, *If I Knew Then What I Know Now*, released in the fall of 2009, journals my experience with a recurrence of cancer and the depression that I faced for the first time in my life as a result of a second battle with this killer disease almost sixteen years after my mother and I fought it side by side. We were diagnosed within days of each other in January 1992. When cancer came back, I was on my own without my strong mother, and it was "The Dash" I turned to when I needed to remind myself what is important.

Life is about what I call the soft skills, and Linda says it best by using words like respect . . . smile . . . slow down . . . and understand how others feel.

If I continue to live my life the way I plan, the dash on my grave marker, many years from now, will translate to two simple words—generous heart. I could ask for no greater gift.

From the heart, with love,
Carol Ann Cole
www.carolanncole.com

The Story of Makayla Joy

I t was the day after Thanksgiving 2009 when I'd heard a tragic story on the news. My heart ached for this family, and I wanted to reach through the TV and somehow comfort the bereaving parents of this beautiful, talented, loving six-year-old little girl who had been murdered in her bed. Her father, a talented TV news photographer, and her devoted mother had taken photos and videos of her throughout her childhood, and I felt a warmth pass through my heart and soul as I viewed them. The genuine love they feel for their daughter and her obvious love of life shine through in every picture, in every video, and you can actually hear her beautiful smile through the words she'd spoken on the recordings.

For reasons I couldn't explain, I was drawn like a magnet to the story of this little girl's "dash." As I learned more about the time she had spent on Earth, I realized why. It wasn't about the length of her life, it was about the love she shared and the effect her legacy still has on others. She had the time of her life during the time of her life. Makayla lived her dash. Today, when I get caught up in insignificant details, I stop and think of her special dash, how precious time is, and what life is really all about. I only wish I'd had the chance to meet her, for I feel my life would be that much more blessed. I like to think she knows she has touched my heart and thus, inspired my words.

While learning about Makayla's dash, I discovered she had a vivid imagination and loved to tell stories. Her parents encouraged her creativity and told her she might be an author one day. Well, today she is! Through the recent release of her storybook, *The Bear's Castle* (available at makaylajoysitton.com), her light continues to shine as all proceeds go directly to the Makayla Joy Sitton Foundation to provide scholarships, so that other children are blessed with the opportunities to enjoy the arts, the way she did.

I received a note from Makayla's father, Jim Sitton. He wrote that my words had helped him cope through the most horrible year of his life. He noted that Makayla lived her dash fully and that my words had encouraged him to do the same. What more could an author require as compensation for their prose?

Makayla's love and spirit remain alive in the hearts of her parents, family, friends, and the many of us who have been, and will continue to be, touched by her dash.

> *"In the end, it's not the years in your life that*
> *matter, it's the life in your years."*
> —Abraham Lincoln

MAKAYLA'S "DASH"
By Jim and Muriel Sitton

Makayla's dash is so many little things—the way she nestled against us on the couch when we read her a story; the lightness of her body when we picked her up and carried her to bed; the smell of her hair; the seriousness with

which she took her piano lessons, her tiny fingers tickling the keys; her little voice as she giggled and told us stories about bears and castles.

Makayla was murdered in her bed on Thanksgiving. It was an act of pure cowardice and evil, and it is easy for those of us who loved her so dearly to feel cheated. There should have been more time. There were more birthday parties to celebrate, more piano recitals, more days at the beach. There should have been graduations, a wedding, and grandchildren. It wasn't fair and it will never make sense. Then again, God is under no obligation to give us all the answers.

But He did entrust us, if only for a while, with an amazing gift: Makayla. And within Makayla's dash, there are many lessons, lessons she taught and continues to teach us about life, about faith, about time—especially time. She seemed somehow to know that time is a divine gift to be treasured and nurtured, not something we are owed or entitled to. This is how she lived. Makayla wanted to learn as much as she could as quickly as possible—she was reading by age two—and she wanted to share everything she learned, whether it was a Bible verse, a song, or a new dance.

Makayla was our only child together. Today, we look through stacks of photographs and seemingly endless video files that are bittersweet reminders of all the little moments we felt the need to capture and preserve. But these images and sounds do more than merely remind us of our precious daughter. They tell a story of her character, and a purpose she was determined to fulfill. We've often described Makayla as "light," a radiance that touches hearts and reaches into cracks and crevices and dark corners. When we see Makayla today, in our memories or in a piece of video, we see her light. She breaths, she lives, and she continues to touch.

Like most little children, Makayla was a tiny package of energy and curiosity. But very early in her life, it was apparent to us that there was something different about her. Perhaps it was a kind of wisdom and perspective that didn't fit such a small person. Makayla didn't watch television and, in fact, she showed no interest. Instead, she read. And read. And read. She also liked to tell stories and we would often tell her she had the makings of a fine author. She had a gift for memorization, particularly when it came to Bible verses and poetry. And as we look back, it's clear that she was teaching us, reaching out to us, shining her light on us.

In some ways, since Makayla's death, time seems to have stood still. Maybe because we are secretly wishing that it [would], in an unprecedented gesture of mercy, reverse course and undo what has been done. Yet, we are constantly reminded that time only knows one direction. Another birthday for Makayla passes, her puppy grows, another Christmas without her. Time continues to do its work, efficiently and without so much as a quick glance over its shoulder. It is drawing our "dash." As Makayla's parents, we are faced with questions and choices. How will we spend our dash? How would Makayla want us to spend it?

There is no such thing as moving on from the death of a child. Coping—yes, healing maybe a little, but never moving on. The void will always be there, and we will deal with it however we can. Little things help and, at the same time, break our hearts. Makayla's mother still lays out her daughter's dresses, not every day like she used to, but two or three times a week. We still set a place for Makayla at breakfast, with her little red cup, her princess placemat, and her two vitamins. There is some comfort in clinging to threads of routine.

But we cannot escape the fact that we too are defining our dash. But will it simply represent the passage of time, the required filling of an empty space, or will the dash between our beginning and end tell a story, a story of life not just lived or endured, but celebrated?

It sounds preposterous to suggest that a six-year-old lived a full life. But how does one define "full"? Makayla's life, short as it was, was more than full; it was bursting at the seams. Makayla's dash is a story, her story. The little piece of punctuation that marks her six years with us is a living, breathing narrative of life, a life of celebration, of love, of victory, of joy. Telling Makayla's story is now our mission and how we will spend our dash. If it is indeed true, as the poem reads, that "what matters most is how we live and love," Makayla had it right. As her parents, we naturally thought we were there for her when, really, she was there for us.

Acknowledgments

This book is a culmination of my life's ideas, thoughts, and experiences thus far and, therefore, could never have been written before this time in my life. All that has happened to me, all that I've learned through my journey and all that I hope my future will bring, I write about. Though not a trained psychologist or a therapist, I am indeed an astute student with a full scholarship to attend what I call Life College. From a unique perspective, I've humbly offered stories and advice on living based on observations that are, though obvious, often overlooked.

Everyone who has played a part in my life, past or present, is responsible for every word I write and for making me into the person I am today. It would be impossible, without omission, to express my gratitude to each and every person whose path I have crossed, be it a positive or negative impression that remained after our time together. It has all . . . in its own way . . . resulted in the "me" I am today.

However, there are some whose love and support encouraged me to follow this dream I tried so hard to ignore, no matter how persistently it would beckon . . .

I begin by offering heartfelt gratitude to my family, whose love and support have provided an indestructible foundation upon which to build my dream. Additionally, I'd like to express honest appreciation to my friends for sharing my words, my work, and my world. I send a sincere and special thank you to my brother Bill and Nancy Shock for encouraging me to stay focused on my goal, and to *Moby in the Morning* for rerouting my journey by reciting my work on the airwaves more than fifteen years ago.

Very special thanks, as well, to my agent, John Willig, who believed in my words of inspiration enough to stand behind them and whose integrity I began to admire from the moment we'd met.

Heartfelt gratitude as well to the editors of Sterling Publishing Co., Inc., for helping translate a rambling poet's vernacular into a more pleasurable reading experience and finding the inadvertent errors made when moments of inspiration overcome grammar skills.

Albert Schweitzer said, "Sometimes our light goes out but is blown again into flame by an encounter with another human being. Each of us owes the deepest thanks to those who have rekindled this inner light." With that in mind, I sincerely thank Mr. Frank Sonnenberg and Ms. Carrie Ralston from Sonnenberg & Partners, for realizing the potential of *Live Your Dash*, designing a new logo, and unknowingly awakening a sleeping giant by reviving and rekindling the energy, enthusiasm, and confidence it took for me to move forward with this project.

Last, but not least, I must acknowledge the contribution of a boss I had when I was young. His name was Larry Gross. Though he'll probably never realize it, his three simple words of advice were successfully heeded more times than I could count. He said to me, "Always Be Yourself." Thanks, Larry, wherever you may be today, for giving me the most honest, useful advice I've ever received.

Being an author is a unique vocation when you truly think about it. People say they are inspired by my words. Technically however, the combinations of vowels and consonants I choose to join together in a certain and specific flow are not "mine." I have merely borrowed and arranged them. The resulting products are considered "mine," though they comprise borrowed components—words that belong to everyone.

I hope that by reading my book you have experienced many moments when you've said to yourself, "I get it." I also hope you will walk away with concepts or ideas that will encourage and inspire you in the days to come to make positive changes, absorb more of life's moments, count your blessings, and . . .

Live Your Dash.

Live Your Dash.

MY LIFE SONG

I ask of you, don't cry for me,
for I have lived my years.
Save the salt and save the water
for those who need your tears.

Instead, celebrate my journey;
lose your sorrow and concern.
We only get one ride in life
and I simply took my turn.

Of myself, I have been proud;
of myself, I've been ashamed,
but through it all, no matter what
I'm the only one I've blamed.

Life's answers weren't always clear
until I looked through aging eyes
at the should've beens . . . the could've beens,
the what if's . . . and the why's.

I've had my joys; I've had my sorrows.
No need for totals or for tallies
of the ups and downs in my life—
I've had more peaks than valleys.

I've had good friends and I've had bad
and I've been both . . . it's true,
for I have lived and loved enough
to have lied . . . and been lied to.

I have fretted; I have stressed
and I have filled my mind with doubt
about the troubles and the problems
that alone, work themselves out.

There are times I would have risen high
if not for my fear of the fall,
but I've learned that feeling pain is better
than feeling nothing there at all.

Sometimes I spent without regard
to the money I was making,
but I always strived in life and love
to give more than I was taking.

I learned late to cherish moments
spent with the many paths I'd crossed
from shedding large, regretful tears
over opportunities I'd lost.

I fell in like and I fell in love.
I gambled and I married.
I was blessed with the health and strength it took
to raise the children I had carried.

Many times I've erred and blundered.
I've made more than my share of mistakes.
I've worried enough to pay in full
the toll that worry takes.

I've always tried to well avoid
confrontation, flack and friction,
but I don't remember hesitating once
to stand up for my convictions.

I've been liked and I've been loathed.
I've been pushed and I've been shoved,
but I say with honesty and gratitude
that I've been truly loved.
At times I've laughed; at times I've cried.
At times I've hoped and prayed.
At times I've regretted the times I worked

those times I should've played.
Sure, there are things I didn't do
and no doubt, things I didn't say,
but if I had one more ticket to ride,
I would ride again today!!

―――――

"If you can only remember me with tears,
then don't remember me at all."

―Walter Breuning at 114 years of age